The Symbolism of
Virginia Woolf

N. C. THAKUR

LONDON
OXFORD UNIVERSITY PRESS
NEW YORK   TORONTO
1965

Oxford University Press, Amen House, London E.C.4

GLASGOW   NEW YORK   TORONTO   MELBOURNE   WELLINGTON
BOMBAY   CALCUTTA   MADRAS   KARACHI   LAHORE   DACCA
CAPE TOWN   SALISBURY   NAIROBI   IBADAN   ACCRA
KUALA LUMPUR   HONG KONG

© Oxford University Press 1965

Printed in Great Britain by
The Camelot Press Ltd., London and Southampton

To

'MERU, SHREE, and MAMMA, Sweet'

Preface

BEING intrigued by *Orlando*, *The Waves* and *Between the Acts*, I started studying the novels of Virginia Woolf seriously about ten years ago. In order to be able to understand her better, I turned to her critics. I found *Virginia Woolf—Her Art as a Novelist* by Joan Bennett, and *Virginia Woolf, a Commentary* by Bernard Blackstone very illuminating. But they left me unsatisfied. W. Y. Tindall's *Forces in Modern British Literature*, and *Virginia Woolf* by David Daiches aroused my interest in her use of symbols. I became convinced that the key to the proper understanding of her novels lay in her symbolism. Not content with the available interpretations of her symbols, I started this study. It has been very rewarding. I have come to appreciate her for the integrity and originality of her mind, for her honest search for the lasting and eternal in the flux and fluidity of life, for her aversion to imposition and exploitation, and for the guidance she gives to a way out of the stress and strife of life.

This study has confirmed me in my belief that she was a daring experimentalist, not an imitator; that she was interested in what G. E. Moore calls 'states of mind', but was nearer to McTaggart and G. L. Dickinson regarding ideas about life and reality; and that she was 'the hostess' of the Bloomsbury Group, but was not of their 'ethos'. She was not, I feel, an 'intellectual' or a philosopher, but a 'seer' and an artist trying to body forth her vision.

I must take this opportunity to express my thanks to the British Council for the award of a travel grant under the Commonwealth University Interchange Scheme to make it possible for me to come to Oxford, and to Dr. T. P. Soper, and through him to the Committee for Commonwealth Studies, for the grant of the Oppenheimer Award to enable me to complete this study.

I am grateful to Mr. J. O. Bayley, Lord David Cecil, Mr. J. B. Bamborough, and Mrs. Joan Bennett for their help, guidance, and valuable suggestions to improve this book. I am indebted to Mr. Leonard Woolf, who very kindly spared time not only to see me and answer all my questions, but also to go through my chapter on *The Waves*. I also owe to him permission to quote from Virginia Woolf's writings. I am grateful to my friend Mr. A. E. Gordon Rudlin for his kindness in reading the proofs.

I have no words to express my gratitude to Professor N. H. K. A. Coghill. I have only this to say that this book owes its very existence to his suggestions, help, and encouragement.

N. C. THAKUR

Linacre House
Oxford

Contents

CHAPTER ONE

Introductory

'SYMBOL' has widely different meanings, and is used for different purposes, in logic, semantics, theology, fine arts, and letters. In literary criticism itself, this term has been used differently by different critics. C. S. Lewis, Maud Bodkin, and C. Day Lewis, for instance, have variously defined symbol. Whereas C. S. Lewis[1] and Maud Bodkin[2] assign different connotations to symbol and allegory, C. Day Lewis differentiates between poetic image and symbol.[3] The Symbolists, as discussed by Arthur Symons, Edmund Wilson, Sir Maurice Bowra, and W. B. Yeats, use symbols to 'spiritualize literature',[4] this movement being 'fundamentally mystical'.[5] To the Symbolists the 'symbolic' means primarily 'a part of the Divine Essence'.[6] They use symbols to create the 'suggestive indefiniteness'[7] that Poe advocated, and choose them arbitrarily as 'a sort of disguise for their ideas'. W. Y. Tindall has tried to make the matter clear by defining the literary symbol as an analogy for something unstated that, going beyond reference and the limits of discourse, embodies and offers a complex of feeling and thought. At the same time, influenced by S. K. Langer, perhaps, he feels that symbol, being 'not entirely translatable and without substitute', resists 'expansion'. He makes the definition vague, I feel, by saying that, as one half of this peculiar analogy embodies the other, 'the symbol is what it symbolizes'.[8]

[1] *The Allegory of Love*, Oxford, 1936, pp. 44–45.
[2] *Archetypal Patterns in Poetry*, London, 1934, p. 204.
[3] *The Poetic Image*, London, 1947, p. 40.
[4] Arthur Symons, *The Symbolist Movement in Literature*, London, 1899, p. 8.
[5] Sir Maurice Bowra, *The Heritage of Symbolism*, London, 1943, p. 2.
[6] W. B. Yeats, 'Symbolism in Painting', *Essays*, London, 1924, p. 183.
[7] Edmund Wilson, *Axel's Castle, A Study in the Imaginative Literature of 1870–1930*, N.Y., 1931, p. 13.
[8] *The Literary Symbol*, N.Y., 1955, pp. 11–13.

My study is neither the nature and scope of symbolism, nor how different movements and different writers have employed it. It is about the symbols used by Virginia Woolf in her novels. By-passing this maze of diverse definitions and uses, therefore, I shall follow the way indicated by her own ideas about the symbol. Though she has not, like A. N. Whitehead, W. M. Urban, E. Cassirer, and S. K. Langer—some of the philosophers interested in symbolism—attempted a systematic study of it, yet she seems to have devoted a good deal of her time and thought to determining its nature and scope. Scattered through-out her critical essays and diary we find a well-thought-out theory of the symbol that compares favourably with the theories of the above-mentioned philosophers whom, as Mr. Leonard Woolf has informed me, she had never read.

A. N. Whitehead in *Symbolism: Its Meaning and Effect* writes that the human mind is said to function symbolically 'when some components of its experience elicit consciousness, beliefs, emotions, and usages respecting other components of its experience'. The former set of components becomes symbol and the latter the meaning of it. He further adds that there must be 'some community between the natures of symbol and its meaning'.[1] S. K. Langer and W. M. Urban, also, insist that there should be some sort of similarity or 'some common logical form'[2] between the symbol and the thing symbolized, otherwise, being unrelated, it would not be a symbol but 'empty imagining'.[3] A. N. Whitehead further points out that 'the object of symbolism is the enhancement of the importance of what it symbolizes'.[4] Virginia Woolf stresses these two points in her essay 'On Not Knowing Greek' which she had written in 1925 long before these philosophers. Comparing Aeschylus and Sophocles she feels that Aeschylus has 'in some mysterious way a general force, a symbolic power'. Explaining his method of achieving this power, she says:

By the bold and running use of metaphor he will amplify and give us, not the thing itself, but the reverberation and reflection which, taken into his mind, the thing has made; close enough to the original

[1] Op. cit., Cambridge, 1928, p. 9.
[2] S. K. Langer, *Feeling and Form*, London, 1953, p. 27.
[3] W. M. Urban, *Language and Reality*, London, 1939, p. 420.
[4] Op. cit., p. 74.

to illustrate it, remote enough to heighten, enlarge, and make
splendid.   (*The Common Reader*, First Series, p. 49)[1]

Thus she points out that a symbol should have some similarity
to the thing symbolized, which it should make splendid. This
enhancement of the importance, and making splendid is
achieved by what Sigmund Freud calls 'condensation' which
makes dreams 'brief, meagre and laconic in comparison with
the range and wealth of the dream-thoughts'.[2] Virginia Woolf
explains it in 'Aurora Leigh', where, comparing the prose
novel to the novel-poem, she remarks:

As we rush through page after page of narrative in which a dozen
scenes that the novelist would smooth out separately are pressed
into one, in which pages of deliberate description are fused into a
single line, we cannot help feeling that the poet has outpaced the
prose writer. Her page is packed twice as full as his. Characters,
too, if they are not shown in conflict but snipped off and summed up
with something of the exaggeration of a caricaturist, have a heightened and symbolical significance which prose with its gradual
approach cannot rival.

                        (*The Common Reader*, Second Series, pp. 212–13)

Virginia Woolf is also of the view that the intuitive realization
that a symbol imparts to us should be instant, because we start
doubting the real and the symbolical if we do not apprehend
symbol and meaning simultaneously. This point she brings out
clearly in her essay on 'The Novels of E. M. Forster'. Comparing the method of Ibsen to that of Forster, she says that
in Forster we get lost, and instead of getting that sense of
instant certainty which we get in *The Wild Duck* or *The Master
Builder*, we are puzzled as to what we ought to understand. This
hesitation, she feels, is fatal. It makes us doubt 'both things—
the real and the symbolical: Mrs. Moore, the nice old lady, and
Mrs. Moore, the sibyl.' Yet a symbol, according to Virginia
Woolf, 'should not cease to be itself by becoming something
else'. It should be 'one single whole', and not appear to us as
'two separate parts'.[3]

---

[1] The quotations from Virginia Woolf's novels, *The Common Reader*,
First and Second Series, *A Room of One's Own*, *The Captain's Death Bed*, and
The Moment and Other Essays are from the Uniform Edition of her works.
[2] *The Interpretation of Dreams*, *The Complete Psychological Works of Sigmund
Freud*, Vol. IV, London, 1953, p. 279.
[3] *The Death of the Moth*, London, 1942, pp. 108–9.

Like W. M. Urban who in *Language and Reality* says that the object of a symbol 'is *suggestion* or *insight* rather than direct or literal representation' (p. 403), Virginia Woolf feels that symbols should not inform but suggest and evoke. Explaining this in her diary, she says:

What interests me most in the last stage is the freedom and boldness with which my imagination picked up, used and tossed aside all images, symbols which I had prepared. I am sure that this is the right way of using them—not in set pieces as I had tried first, coherently, simply as images, never making them work out; only suggest.[1]

She rightly feels that insight symbols, if used in set pieces, losing originality and evocative power, become faded metaphors.

Virginia Woolf's admission that she 'prepared' symbols, as evidenced by the quotation above, clarifies the nature of her symbols. Mostly they are not, like Freud's dream symbols or Jung's archetypes, the product of the unconscious. In his commentary on *The Secret of the Golden Flower* Jung says that symbols are the result of a psychic process of development and not of rational thinking. Freud, talking about symbols in *The Interpretation of Dreams*, calls them 'unconscious ideation'.[2] Virginia Woolf's symbols are aesthetic symbols rationally created to suggest and give insight into the ineffable in human thought and feeling, or to heighten and make splendid the desired emotions and ideas; hence they are easy to interpret in the light of the thoughts and feelings that are available in her literary criticism, diary, and other writings.

Virginia Woolf not only has stated the nature of the symbol but also has tried to explain how it works and affects our minds, how it gives us insight into things, and reveals in a flash the depths of its meaning. Writing on 'Pictures', she says:

Here is a scene in a theatre, for example. We have to understand the emotions of a young man for a lady in a box below. With an abundance of images and comparisons we are made to appreciate the forms, the colours, the very fibre and texture of the plush seats and the ladies' dresses and the dullness or glow, sparkle or colour,

---

[1] *A Writer's Diary*, London, 1954, p. 101. (This book will in future be referred to as *Diary*.)

[2] *The Complete Psychological Works of Sigmund Freud*, Vol. V, p. 351.

of the light. At the same time that our senses drink in all this our minds are tunnelling logically and intellectually into the obscurity of the young man's emotions, which as they ramify and modulate and stretch further and further, at last penetrate too far, peter out into such a shred of meaning that we can scarcely follow any more, were it not that suddenly in flash after flash, metaphor after metaphor, the eye lights up that cave of darkness and we are shown hard tangible material shapes of bodiless thoughts hanging like bats in the primeval darkness where light has never visited them before.

(*The Moment and Other Essays*, p. 141)

Similarly explaining in her essay 'De Quincey's Autobiography' how the mind of a reader is affected, she writes:

If we try to analyse our sensations we shall find that we are worked upon as if by music—the senses are stirred rather than the brain. The rise and fall of the sentence immediately soothes us to a mood and removes us to a distance in which the near fades and detail is extinguished ..... The emotion is never stated; it is suggested and brought slowly by repeated images before us until it stays, in all its complexity, complete.

(*The Common Reader*, Second Series, pp. 133–4)

Thus she explains how repeated images, working on our senses by suggesting emotions and ideas, become symbolic. Character, atmosphere, and action, too, she feels, have symbolic value. Writing about George Meredith, she says that he brings forward 'the sea or the sky or the wood' to symbolize what 'the human beings are feeling or looking'. She further adds:

He is among the poets who identify the character with the passion or with the idea; who symbolise and make abstract.

(*The Common Reader*, Second Series, pp. 231–2)

Talking about 'The Novels of Thomas Hardy', also, she says that his characters, besides representing 'fellow-beings driven by their own passions and idiosyncrasies', have 'something symbolical' about them.

Besides character and atmosphere, she has mentioned actions that attain symbolic value. Writing about Tolstoy in 'The Russian Point of View', she says that

what his infallible eye reports of a cough or a trick of the hands his infallible brain refers to something hidden in the character, so that we know his people, not only by the way they love and their views on politics and the immortality of the soul, but also by the way they sneeze and choke. (*The Common Reader*, First Series, p. 229)

The coughing and the trick of the hand, the sneezing and choking, suggesting something hidden in the characters, become symbolic actions.

Virginia Woolf not only has stated the nature and scope of the symbol, but also has explained why we need it. She seems to believe with E. Cassirer that man is not 'animal rationale' but is 'animal symbolicum'.[1] Like A. N. Whitehead, who says that 'Mankind has to find a symbol to express himself', she writes:

We grasp what is beyond their surface meaning, gather instinctively this, that, and the other—a sound, a colour, here a stress, there a pause—which the poet, knowing words to be meagre in comparison with ideas, has strewn about his page to evoke, when collected, a state of mind which neither words can express nor the reason explain.[2]

That we need symbols, because words are meagre in comparison with ideas, she has stressed in another essay also. In ' "Jane Eyre" and "Wuthering Heights" ' she explains how the untamed ferocity, which is perpetually at war with the accepted order of things, makes the Brontës 'desire to create instantly rather than to observe patiently'. They, therefore, she adds, 'feel the need of some powerful symbol of the vast and slumbering passions in human nature than words or actions can convey'.[3]

Virginia Woolf, it can now be deduced, is of the view that when a writer desires to express some genuinely new ideas or states of mind which he cannot adequately convey through the stiff and conventional medium of language in its literal capacity, he uses character, action, atmosphere, images to 'evoke' and suggest them; and that these images, acquiring added significance, become symbols.

To suggest her inscapes and to evoke her instresses, therefore, Virginia Woolf, like James Joyce, D. H. Lawrence, André Gide, Thomas Mann, Franz Kafka and William Faulkner,

---

[1] *An Essay on Man*, Yale, 1944, p. 25.
[2] *On Being Ill*, London, 1930, p. 27.
[3] *The Common Reader*, First Series, pp. 200–1.

makes an abundant use of symbols. Unlike Wells, Bennett, and Galsworthy, whom she calls 'materialists', Virginia Woolf is not interested in describing a very solid and substantial 'Mrs. Brown' with the brooch and gloves that she wore and the place and society she belonged to, but desires to convey what Mrs. Brown *is*: a symbol of 'the spirit we live by, life itself'.[1] That Virginia Woolf was preoccupied with what life and reality is is evident from the testimony of her friends, from her own remarks that she has recorded in her diary, and from the thoughts and utterances of most of her characters who ask questions about life and its meaning. Rachel in *The Voyage Out* (p. 145) questions, 'And life, what was that?' Clarissa in *Mrs. Dalloway* (p. 143) tries to find out 'What did it mean to her, this thing called life?' Similarly Bernard and Louis in *The Waves* (pp. 84 and 165), in order to understand life and personality, question, 'What am I?' and 'Who are you?' William Bankes in *To the Lighthouse* questions 'Is life this?' (p. 139), and Eleanor in *The Years* thinks 'there must be another life' (p. 461). Some of the utterances of these characters reproduce the exact phrases used by Virginia Woolf in her diary. 'More and more do I repeat,' she records in her diary, 'my own version of Montaigne—"It's life that matters."'[2] In *Night and Day* (p. 132) Katharine Hilbery, like her creator, while walking, along the Strand goes on 'repeating to herself some lines which had stuck in her memory: "It's life that matters, nothing but life ....."' At another place Virginia Woolf writes, 'Who am I, what am I, and so on: these questions are always floating about in me .....'[3] and these words are echoed by Louis: 'What do I think of you—what do you think of me? Who are you? Who am I?' E. M. Forster, who knew Virginia Woolf personally, says in his Rede Lecture on her, 'She was full of interests, and their number increased as she grew older, she was curious about life, and she was tough, sensitive but tough.'[4] This 'life that matters',[5] and about which she was curious, is for her 'the oddest affair; has in it the essence of reality'.[6] Life or spirit, this the essential thing, for Virginia Woolf '..... is a luminous halo, a

---

[1] *Mr. Bennett and Mrs. Brown*, London, 1924, p. 24.
[2] *Diary*, p. 72.   [3] Ibid., p. 86.
[4] *Virginia Woolf*, Cambridge, 1942, p. 5.
[5] *Diary*, p. 72.   [6] Ibid., p. 101.

semi-transparent envelope'.[1] In its manifested form Virginia
Woolf saw life, like Spenser, Keats, and Walter Pater, as something ever changing, mutable, and protean. Consequently, to
convey her vision of this unknown and uncircumscribed spirit,
and protean life, she feels the need of using symbols abun-
dantly.

Thoughts and ideas, like concepts of life and reality, are
intangible, shapeless things which demand symbols to make
them palpable and comprehensible. *Jacob's Room*, *Mrs.
Dalloway*, *To the Lighthouse*, *Orlando* and *The Waves*, besides
portraying what Elizabeth Bowen calls the 'intense inner
existence'[2] of the characters, are, as Virginia Woolf herself
implies, novels of idea.[3] Therefore, to convey successfully her
ideas about modern civilization, intellect and intuition, time,
change, and eternity, and life, personality, and consciousness,
she has used more symbols in these novels. *The Waves*, which is,
as she herself says, a 'serious, mystical, poetical work',[4] and in
which she tried to come to terms with her 'mystical feelings',[5]
is highly symbolical. Its characters, who appear to day-dream
aloud, also use condensed and symbolical language.

Virginia Woolf's characters, like their author, have their
visions and dreams. Rachel and Hewet in *The Voyage Out*,
Ralph, Katharine, and Mary in *Night and Day*, Lily in *To the
Lighthouse*, and Peggy and Sara in *The Years*, are some of the
characters who under stresses of acute agony and emotional
agitation have visions, and try to suggest them through
symbols. For instance, when Ralph has to suggest a 'confused
and emotional moment' of life, he resorts to drawing a symbolical central blot surrounded by a circumference of smudges.[6]

Another, and perhaps the most important, reason why
Virginia Woolf made a frequent use of symbols is the fact that
she was constantly subjected to illnesses, acute influenza, and
violent headaches. Long drawn-out illnesses, like highly emotional stresses, have a great sensitizing effect on the mind. They
often make people clairvoyant. It was in her illnesses, which she
felt were partly mystical, that she saw her books in their ideal
state. Explaining this in her diary, she says:

[1] *The Common Reader*, First Series, p. 189.
[2] *English Novelists*, London, 1942, p. 48.   [3] *Diary*, p. 189.
[4] Ibid., p. 105.   [5] Ibid., p. 137.   [6] *Night and Day*, pp. 514–15.

Once or twice I have felt that odd whirr of wings in the head, which comes when I am ill so often—last year for example at this time I lay in bed constructing *A Room of One's Own* ..... If I could stay in bed another fortnight ..... I believe I should see the whole of *The Waves*. (p. 153)

She has also explained in her diary how 'one becomes fertilised' in times of illnesses which 'are the most fruitful artistically' (p. 146).

Something happens in my mind. It refuses to go on registering impressions. It shuts itself up. It becomes chrysalis. I lie quite torpid, often with acute physical pain ..... Then suddenly something springs ..... ideas rush in me; often though this is before I can control my mind or pen. (*Diary*, pp. 153-4)

Such ideas as spring up suddenly mostly express themselves in symbols. W. B. Yeats, who was deeply interested in the occult, and who used to practise meditation writes in his essay, 'The Symbolism of Poetry':

the soul moves among symbols and unfolds in symbols when trance, or madness, or deep meditation has withdrawn it from every impulse but its own.[1]

Her illnesses not only supplied her ideas, but also showed her the 'mystic quality' of words—what lay 'beyond their surface meaning'.[2] This symbolic and evocative power of words was useful to Virginia Woolf in externalizing her visions, genuinely new ideas, and states of mind, which were difficult to communicate in direct statements without the loss of their aesthetic value.

One of the sayings of the Alchemists, as reported by C. G. Jung in *Psychology and Alchemy*, is: 'For those who have the symbol the passage is easy.'[3] Agreeing with the Alchemists, I feel that the understanding of Virginia Woolf's novels becomes easier, and the enjoyment of them greater, if we realize the significance of her symbols. In pointing out the symbols in her novels I have tried not to be arbitrary, but to give reasons for so labelling them. In distinguishing what

[1] W. B. Yeats, *Essays*, p. 199.   [2] *On Being Ill*, 1930, p. 27.
[3] *The Collected Works of C. G. Jung*, Vol. 12, London, 1953, p. 215. It is a translation of an Alchemical *verbum magistri* from Mylius which reads, 'Habentibus symbolum facilis est transitus.'

W. M. Urban calls, 'the symbolic from the literal meaning', and in developing their 'unexpressed reference',[1] I have quoted, sometimes, at length from her writings. To determine the truth and validity of her symbols, and thus to enrich and deepen their meanings, I have compared them, as far as possible, to the symbols used by other writers, especially poets and mystics, for she was a mystic poet herself in spite of the medium that she used.

[1] *Language and Reality*, p. 428.

CHAPTER TWO

The Voyage Out *and*
Night and Day

VIRGINIA WOOLF'S first two novels, *The Voyage Out* and *Night and Day*, according to her own classification are novels of fact. With carefully thought out plots, cleverly contrived incidents, and well delineated characters, these are, as Katherine Mansfield says, 'in the tradition of the English novel'.[1] In contrast to Jacob Flanders in *Jacob's Room*, Clarissa Dalloway in *Mrs. Dalloway*, Mrs. Ramsay in *To the Lighthouse*, and Bernard in *The Waves*, whose characters one gleans from their thoughts and feelings or from the thoughts and reactions of other characters (which perhaps made Arnold Bennett write that Virginia Woolf could not create character,[2] and Arthur Compton-Rickett say that her characters had 'no more substance than ghosts'[3]), the characters of Willoughby, Rachel, and Dalloway in *The Voyage Out*, and of Mr. Hilbery, Katharine, and Mary in *Night and Day*, are delineated in the conventional manner of Jane Austen, George Eliot, H. G. Wells, and Arnold Bennett. For instance, if we compare the character-sketch of Katharine in *Night and Day* with that of Harriet in *Emma*, the similarity of style becomes apparent. Describing Harriet, Jane Austen says:

She was short, plump and fair, with a fine bloom, blue eyes, light hair, regular features, and a look of great sweetness; and before the ending of the evening, Emma was as much pleased with her manner as her person .....

She was not struck by any thing remarkably clever in Miss [Harriet] Smith's conversation, but she found her altogether very engaging—not inconveniently shy, not unwilling to talk—and yet

---

[1] *Novels and Novelists*, London, 1930, p. 111.
[2] *The Savour of Life*, London, 1928, p. 48.
[3] *Portraits and Personalities*, London, 1937, p. 76.

so far from pushing, shewing so proper and becoming a deference,
seeming so pleasantly grateful for being admitted to Hartfield, and
so artlessly impressed by the appearance of every thing in so superior
a style to what she had been used to, that she must have good sense
and deserve encouragement.[1]

Virginia Woolf, delineating the character of Katharine, writes:

She had the quick, impulsive movements of her mother, the lips
parting often to speak, and closing again; and the dark oval eyes of
her father brimming with light upon a basis of sadness, or, since she
was too young to have acquired a sorrowful point of view, one might
say that the basis was not sadness so much as a spirit given to contemplation and self-control. Judging by her hair, her colouring, and
the shape of her features, she was striking, if not actually beautiful.
Decision and composure stamped her, a combination of qualities
that produced a very marked character, and one that was not
calculated to put a young man, who scarcely knew her, at his ease.
For the rest, she was tall; her dress was of some quiet colour, with
old yellow-tinted lace for ornament, to which the spark of an ancient
jewel gave its one red gleam.   (*Night and Day*, p. 5)

Both Jane Austen and Virginia Woolf, by mentioning the
features, colour of eyes and hair, and the bodily build of Harriet
and Katharine, have created word pictures of them. But whereas
Jane Austen lays stress on the social manners and the sense
of propriety of Harriet, Virginia Woolf emphasizes Katharine's
mental qualities and their inner springs.

The Voyage Out and *Night and Day*, like *Emma*, *Middlemarch*,
The Old Wives' Tale, *Marriage*, and *The Longest Journey*, are
concerned with portraying human relationships, especially
love and marriage. In *The Voyage Out* Rachel Vinrace, while
talking to Mrs. Dalloway, innocently inquires, 'Why do people
marry?' Mrs. Dalloway laughingly replies, 'That's what you're
going to find out' (p. 64). It is Rachel again who asks Evelyn,
'What d'you think its like ..... being in love?' (p. 306).
Rachel's very life is a voyage out to find the reality about love
and life and marriage. Hewet and Helen, also, like Rachel, Mrs.
Dalloway, and Evelyn, talk about love and marriage (pp. 294–5
and 351–2). Similarly in *Night and Day* Katharine and Ralph
have their doubts about love and marriage: Ralph at one
time thinks that love is 'madness, romance, hallucination'

[1] *Emma*, Oxford Illustrated Jane Austen, 1926, p. 23.

(p. 409), as if when they think that they are in love they are but imagining a thing that does not exist. It is Mrs. Hilbery who feels that marriage is a school, and that 'you don't get the prizes unless you go to school' (p. 221). She insists, 'Don't marry unless you are in love.' Because she believes that 'the best of life is built on what we say when we're in love'. 'It isn't nonsense, Katharine,' she says, 'it's the truth, it's the only truth' (p. 324).

In the pairing of its characters for marriage, too, *Night and Day* follows a traditional pattern. It is more akin to *Emma* in this respect than to any other novel mentioned above. In *Emma*, Harriet on refusing Martin gets attached to Mr. Elton; then she is supposed to be in love with Frank, and afterwards with Mr. Knightley, but ultimately she marries Martin. Emma herself attracts Mr. Elton, is attracted by Frank, but finally finding herself in love with Mr. Knightley marries him. Similarly in *Night and Day* Katharine is engaged to Rodney, but breaking that engagement marries Ralph. Ralph proposes to Mary, is refused by her, and marries Katharine. Rodney is first engaged to Katharine, then falls in love with Cassandra, turns away from her and wants to marry Katharine; on being refused by Katharine, he is happy to marry Cassandra.

Thus concerned in presenting a conventional theme in the traditional style, Virginia Woolf in *The Voyage Out* and *Night and Day* employs atmosphere, character, and action as symbols mostly in the traditional way. Even so, she is obliged to use symbols in a subtler way when she has to suggest the highly emotional state of mind of her characters or to evoke their feelings and thoughts.

The titles of both the novels are suggestive. The voyage from London in England to Santa Marina in South America, besides being a physical voyage out for Rachel, Hirst, Hewet, and Susan, is a voyage out into the world of love and adventure. For Hirst it was a voyage out 'to settle the matter' (p. 189) whether he was going to the Bar or to Cambridge; for Susan it was a voyage out from 'the long solitude of an old maid's life' (p. 162) into the world of romance and marriage, and for Rachel, who had lived a secluded life under the protection of old aunts, it was a voyage out into the world of experience and comprehension of life. Rachel's going out from the misty and cold London to the dazzling, sparkling heat of South America symbolizes her growing out of her cool and unsensuous girl-hood into warm and sensuous maidenhood. She was, as Helen thought, 'an unlicked girl' (p. 18) with a 'hesitation in speaking, or rather a tendency to use the wrong words' which 'made her seem more than normally incompetent for her years' (pp. 14–15). This innocent and ignorant girl, who at the age of twenty-four scarcely knew 'that men desired women' (p. 90), becomes conscious of life and love when she first experiences Mr. Dalloway's kiss and then Hewet's love for her. Like Dorothy Richardson's *Pilgrimage* which is a pilgrimage of Miriam Henderson's mind from adolescence to middle age, this voyage out becomes a symbol of Rachel's growing and going out into the world, of her facing life as it is, and finally, perhaps, as suggested by Dorothy Brewster and Angus Burrell, of her 'voyage out of life altogether'.[1]

In the same way *Night and Day* not only suggests Rodney's fluctuating affections for Katharine and Cassandra, but also symbolizes the varying joy and dismay that Katharine and Ralph experience during their uncertainty. When Ralph goes to tell Mary that he is in love with Katharine, he says,

I suppose I'm in love. Anyhow, I'm out of my mind. I can't think, I can't work, I don't care a hang for anything in the world. Good Heavens, Mary! I'm in torment. One moment I'm happy; next I'm miserable. I hate her for half an hour; then I'd give my whole life to be with her for ten minutes; all the time I don't know what I feel, or why I feel it; it's insanity, and yet it's perfectly reasonable.

(*Night and Day*, p. 413)

While talking to Mrs. Hilbery, Katharine expresses similar feelings:

It seems ..... as if something came to an end suddenly—gave out—faded—an illusion—as if when we think we're in love we make it up—we imagine what doesn't exist ..... Always to be finding the other an illusion, and going off and forgetting about them, never to be certain that you cared, or that he wasn't caring for some one not you at all, the horror of changing from one state to the other, being happy one moment and miserable the next.

(*Night and Day*, pp. 512–13)

[1] *Modern Fiction*, N.Y., 1934, p. 234.

Portraying thus the shifting relationships of the characters, and their changing moods from misery to happiness, *Night and Day* becomes a symbol of the night and day of their feelings and emotions.

Virginia Woolf, like the Brontës, George Meredith, and Thomas Hardy, employs atmosphere and landscape symbolically to suggest the states of mind and to evoke the feelings of her characters. In *The Voyage Out* the cold and misty atmosphere of London with the 'fine rain', the obliterating 'fine yellow fog' and 'a certain amount of troubled yellow light' on a river running with 'great force' (pp. 4–6) becomes an apt symbol of the gloom and misery that Helen Ambrose was feeling on leaving her children behind.

After the first uncomfortable night on board the *Euphrosyne*

..... the breakfast next morning wore a kind of beauty. The voyage had begun, and had begun happily with a soft blue sky, and a calm sea ..... The table was cheerful with apples and bread and eggs ..... They were free of roads, free of mankind, and the same exhilaration at their freedom ran through them all. The ship was making her way steadily through small waves which slapped her and then fizzled like effervescing water, leaving a little border of bubbles and foam on either side.   (*The Voyage Out*, pp. 19, 23)

The soft blue sky and the calm sea become symbols of the peaceful state of mind of the passengers on the boat, and the effervescing water and the bubbles and foam, of the exhilaration experienced by them.

As Shakespeare in *King Lear* employs the blowing and raging winds, the cataracts and hurricanes, the sulphurous fires, and the oak-cleaving thunderbolts, in order to suggest, what Lear calls, 'the tempest in my mind', Virginia Woolf uses storm not only to create an occasion for Richard Dalloway to kiss Rachel, but also to symbolize his passion, as well as her feelings aroused by her first impact as a woman with a man:

Even at tea the floor rose beneath their feet and pitched too low again, and at dinner the ship seemed to groan and strain as though a lash were descending. She who had been a broad-backed dray-horse, upon whose hind-quarters pierrots might waltz, became a colt in the fields .....

Next morning the storm was on them, and no politeness could ignore it ..... For comfort they retreated to their cabins, where with tightly wedged feet they let the ship bounce and tumble. Their sensations were the sensations of potatoes in a sack on a galloping horse.   (*The Voyage Out*, pp. 77–78)

The rising and pitching low of the floor of the ship with its groans and strains, the turning of the dray-horse into a colt in the fields, and the bouncing and tumbling like potatoes in a sack on a galloping horse, are apt symbols of the character and state of mind of Rachel who, on being kissed by Mr. Dalloway, felt 'tremendous beats of the heart, each of which sent black waves across her eyes' (p. 84).

Similarly, when, standing in 'a whirlpool of wind' with papers 'flying round in circles', Mr. Dalloway exclaims, 'My word! What a tempest!', the tempest becomes a macrocosm of his mind. He was unable to resist the 'inestimable power' of Rachel's beauty. Holding her tight in his arms, therefore, he 'kissed her passionately' (pp. 83–84).

Rachel's death in the prime of her life, and within a couple of weeks after her engagement to Hewet, affects all.

'Rachel! Rachel!' he shrieked, trying to rush back to her. But they prevented him, and pushed him down the passage and into a bedroom far from her room. Downstairs they could hear the thud of his feet on the floor, as he struggled to break free; and twice they heard him shout, 'Rachel, Rachel!'   (p. 432)

The people at the hotel, too, like Hewet and the others at the villa, were feeling her death acutely:

At about half-past nine Miss Allan came very slowly into the hall, and walked very slowly to the table ..... she stood still, thinking, with her head a little sunk upon her shoulders ..... She looked up to see Mrs. Thornbury standing beside her, with lines drawn upon her forehead, and her lips parted as if she was about to ask a question ..... Mrs. Thornbury made a little exclamation, drew her lips together, and the tears rose in her eyes ..... It was evident that Evelyn had been lately in tears, and when she looked at Mrs. Thornbury she began to cry again.   (pp. 434–5)

These statements describe only the outer expression of grief. In order to give us a peep into the inner commotion of the characters and to portray their tense emotions which were like those of Catherine on the disappearance of Heathcliff in

Wuthering Heights, Virginia Woolf, in the manner of Emily Brontë, uses storm symbolically:

> All that evening the clouds gathered, until they closed entirely over the blue of the sky. They seemed to narrow the space between earth and heaven, so that there was no room for the air to move in freely; and the waves, too, lay flat, and yet rigid, as if they were restrained. The leaves on the bushes and trees in the garden hung closely together, and the feeling of pressure and restraint was increased by the short chirping sounds which came from birds and insects ..... The first roll of thunder and the first heavy drop striking the pane caused a little stir ..... There was then a profound silence ..... followed by a clap of thunder right over the hotel. The rain swished with it, and immediately there were all those sounds of windows being shut and doors slamming violently which accompany a storm.
>
> The room grew suddenly several degrees darker, for the wind seemed to be driving waves of darkness across the earth ..... The flashes now came frequently, lighting up faces as if they were to be photographed, surprising them in tense and unnatural expressions.
>
> (pp. 449–50)

The gathering clouds, the suffocating air, the rigid flat waves, the pressure and restraint of the cloud about to burst, and then the rolling thunder, the swishing rain, and the flashing lightning illuminating the tense and unnatural expressions in the spreading waves of darkness, symbolize the feelings and mental states which the characters experienced during Rachel's illness and on her death, and which could not be conveyed adequately by describing their outer reactions.

Besides employing storm, as did Shakespeare and Emily Brontë, to symbolize emotions and states of mind, Virginia Woolf uses it to suggest her idea about life and death. By Rachel's death in *The Voyage Out* Virginia Woolf does not mean, as Brimley Johnson thinks, to concede 'to the prevailing taste for tragedy',[1] nor 'to create a meretricious sympathy for her and a meretricious solution of her problem',[2] nor does it mean that Virginia Woolf is considering death, in this instance, as the great unifier, which Irma Rantavaara, thinking of T. S.

---

[1] *Some Contemporary Novelists* (women), London, 1920, p. 157.
[2] Edwin Berry Burgum, *The Novel and the World's Dilemma*, N.Y., 1947, p. 125.

Eliot's 'In my end is my beginning', takes it to mean.[1] She introduces death, as she described to Lytton Strachey,

..... to give the feeling of a vast tumult of life, as various and dis-orderly as possible, which should be cut short for a moment by the death, and go on again—and the whole was to have a sort of pattern, and be somehow controlled.[2]

The storm, like death, had made everyone uneasy and gloomy; it had made them feel tense and restrained, and had brought life to a standstill: leaving all other business they had 'collected in little groups' (p. 450). But after a minute or two, when the storm drew away and the atmosphere became lighter, the people in the hall of the hotel sat down. They began to tell each other stories about great storms. In many cases they produced 'their occupation for the evening'.

The chess-board was brought out ..... Round them gathered a group of ladies with pieces of needlework, or in default of needlework, with novels ..... Mrs. Paley just round the corner had her cards arranged in long ladders before her ..... and the merchants and the miscellan-eous people who had never been discovered to possess names were stretched in their arm-chairs with their newspapers on their knees.
(pp. 451-2)

In the same way different people got busy in different ways after the news of Rachel's death: Arthur started a completely new topic of conversation; Arthur and Susan congratulated Hugling Elliot upon his convalescence; Mr. Perrott asked Evelyn to meet him in the garden (pp. 442-4). This is what Virginia Woolf meant by the going on of life again after being cut short for a moment by death. Thus the storm attains symbolic value, producing the same effect as death.

Writing about the novels of George Meredith in 1928, Virginia Woolf says:

It is significant that Richard and Lucy, Harry and Ottilia, Clara and Vernon, Beauchamp and Renée are presented in carefully appro-priate surroundings—on board a yacht, under a flowering cherry tree, upon some river-bank, so that the landscape always makes part of the emotion. The sea or the sky or the wood is brought forward to symbolise what the human beings are feeling or looking.
(*The Common Reader*, Second Series, p. 231)

---

[1] *Virginia Woolf and Bloomsbury*, Helsinki, 1953, p. 86.
[2] *Virginia Woolf and Lytton Strachey: Letters*, London, 1956, p. 57.

She herself had employed this method of using landscape and natural surroundings symbolically as early as 1915 in *The Voyage Out*. When Rachel and Hewet, leaving Helen and Hirst in the garden, go out for a walk, they reach 'the edge of the cliff where, looking down into the sea, you might chance on jelly-fish and dolphins'.

Rachel lay down on her elbow, and parted the tall grasses which grew on the edge, so that she might have a clear view. The water was very calm; rocking up and down at the base of the cliff, and so clear that one could see the red of the stones at the bottom of it. So it had been at the birth of the world, and so it had remained ever since. Probably no human being had ever broken that water with boat or with body.   (pp. 249–50)

The calm and clear water of the sea lying untouched by boat or body becomes a symbol of the peace and clarity of their minds. It was there that Rachel for the first time realized 'with a great sense of comfort how easily she could talk to Hewet, those thorns or ragged corners which tear the surface of some relationships being smoothed away' (p. 252). And it was there also that Hewet became clear about the depth of his feeling for Rachel, whose body 'far from being unattractive was very attractive to him', and whom he wanted to hold in his arms. In this pastoral setting when Rachel suddenly observes, 'I like you, d'you like me?', Hewet feels relieved to say, what he wanted to say, 'I like you immensely'. This mood of sudden rush of delight Virginia Woolf again symbolizes by the change in the sky-scape:

The substantial blue day had faded to a paler and more ethereal blue; the clouds were pink, far away and closely packed together; and the peace of evening had replaced the heat of the southern afternoon, in which they had started on their walk.   (p. 265)

Whereas the paler and more ethereal blue suggests the mellow-ness of their feelings, the closely packed pink clouds seem to represent the ardent desire in their hearts.

'Sweet are the shy recesses of the woodlands', says Meredith in *The Ordeal of Richard Feverel*, because there 'From silence into silence things move.' Terence and Rachel, leaving Helen, Hirst, and the Flushings, go out for a walk into the wood:

tropical bushes with their sword-like leaves grew at the side, and the ground was covered with an unmarked springy moss instead of grass, starred with little yellow flowers. As they passed into the depths of the forest the light grew dimmer ..... The path narrowed and turned; it was hedged in by dense creepers which knotted tree to tree, and burst here and there into star-shaped crimson blossoms ..... The atmosphere was close and the air came at them in languid puffs of scent ..... Not only did the silence weigh upon them, but they were both unable to frame any thoughts.   (p. 331)

The profound silence in the dense depths of the forest thick with tropical bushes becomes an apt symbol of their inarticulate emotions and desires, which ultimately find expression and utterance in their clasping each other in their arms, and in muttering, 'We love each other.' (p. 332)

In *Night and Day*, also, Virginia Woolf makes use of atmosphere and landscape to symbolize the states of mind and the emotional reactions of the characters in the novel. George Eliot in *Middlemarch*, when describing Sir James's reactions to the news of Miss Brooke's engagement to Casaubon, tells how he had a 'deeply-hurt expression' on his face 'which he was trying to conceal by a nervous smile, while he whipped his boot', how he 'let his whip fall and stooped to pick it up', and how, after handing Mrs. Cadwallader, who had conveyed the disturbing news, to the phaeton, he jumped on his horse since he was not going 'to renounce his ride because of his friend's unpleasant news'.[1] Whereas George Eliot describes the outward expressions only, Virginia Woolf, in describing a similar situation, tries to give us an insight into Ralph Denham's mind, and to show his agitated feelings. When Ralph Denham comes to know that 'Katharine's engaged to William Rodney', he leaves the house and strides with extreme swiftness along the Embankment.

..... He felt himself now, as he had often fancied other people, adrift on the stream, and far removed from control of it, a man with no grasp upon circumstances any longer ..... He felt for corners of his being untouched by his disaster; but there was no limit to the flood of damage; not one of his possessions was safe now ..... He sat himself down, in spite of the chilly fog which obscured the farther bank and

[1] Book I, Vol. I, London, 1910, p. 83.

left its lights suspended upon a blank surface, upon one of the river-side seats, and let the tide of disillusionment sweep through him ..... He rose, and looked into the river, whose swift race of dun-coloured waters seemed the very spirit of futility and oblivion ..... He did not blame her; he blamed nothing, nobody; he saw the truth. He saw the dun-coloured race of waters and the blank shore.

(Night and Day, pp. 162-3)

Trying to lay more stress on the inner mental turmoil than on the outer physical expressions, Virginia Woolf uses the obscuring chilly fog, the swift race of dun-coloured waters, and the blank shore, to suggest symbolically the state of Ralph's confused tumultuous mind. The obscuring chilly fog not only suggests the benumbing pain that had flooded his whole being and taken possession 'of every governing seat', but also evokes the bleakness of future that he felt on seeing his 'old romance' come to an end and the substantial world, with its prospect of avenues leading on and on, slipping away from him. Similarly the swift race of dun-coloured waters, besides suggesting the rushing on of his life towards oblivion, symbolizes the turbid tumult of his feelings of rage, pain, and disillusionment, and his sensations of exhaustion, lack of control, and of being 'adrift on the stream'.

On another occasion in *Night and Day* Rodney, who is staying at Stogdon House during Christmas week, feels slighted and is angry with Katharine. He seeks an opportunity to speak to her. Therefore, on their way back from Lincoln they get down from the carriage about two miles from Lampsher near a lonely heath.

In summer it was a pleasant place, for the deep woods on either side murmured, and the heather, which grew thick round the granite pedestal, made the light breeze taste sweetly; in winter the sighing of the trees was deepened to a hollow sound, and the heath was as grey and almost as solitary as the empty sweep of the clouds above it.   (p. 249)

The wintry scene with sighing trees and prevailing greyness appropriately reflects their depressed mood, and the lack of warmth and colour in their feelings at that particular moment of their life. There, when Rodney implores her to say that she cares for him, she could not force herself to speak a word. The heather was going dim around them, and the horizon was blotted out by white mist.

This dim misty atmosphere, as Virginia Woolf herself hints in the following sentence, becomes a symbol of Katharine's damp feelings towards Rodney:

To ask her for passion or for certainty seemed like asking that damp prospect for fierce blades of fire, or the faded sky for the intense blue vault of June.   (p. 253)

The 'scattering of dead leaves all round them which had been blown by the wind into heaps, a foot or two deep, here and there', that Katharine notices while explaining her feelings reflects the nature of her emotion for Rodney—it is dead and withered. Farther on she says:

'You don't understand, I mean, my real feelings; how could you? I've only now faced them myself. But I haven't got the sort of feeling—love, I mean—I don't know what to call it'—she looked vaguely towards the horizon sunk under mist—'but, anyhow, without it our marriage would be a farce —'   (pp. 256-7)

The horizon sunk under mist towards which she looks vaguely appears to her as a symbol of the farce that her marriage would be if she married without having any love for Rodney. It would be all mist without any ray of hope or any bright spot to look forward to.

In contrast Kew Gardens with 'the lake, the broad green spaces, the vista of trees, with the ruffled gold of the Thames in the distance' on a warm afternoon in the first of spring, becomes an appropriate setting suggestive of the warm youthful feelings of Katharine and Ralph. While they sat there upon a seat in a glade of beech-trees,

Denham was engaged in uncovering with the point of his stick a group of green spikes half smothered by the dead leaves. He did this with the peculiar touch of the botanist ..... She then asked him to inform her about flowers. To her they were variously shaped and coloured petals, poised, at different seasons of the year, upon very similar green stalks; but to him they were, in the first instance, bulbs or seeds, and later, living things endowed with sex, and pores, and susceptibilities which adapted themselves by all manner of ingenious devices to live and beget life ..... No discourse could have

worn a more welcome sound in Katharine's ears ..... It wakened
echoes in all those remote fastnesses of her being where loneliness
had brooded so long undisturbed.   (pp. 348–50)

The uncovering by Ralph of the green spikes half smothered
by the dead leaves becomes symbolic of the awaking in her of
the life impulse—sex, companionship, and human understanding—which she lacked so long as she was interested in Mathematics and Astronomy—figures, laws, stars, and facts—which
had been the only things in whose reality she could believe
(p. 229), and which was now quickened by his discourse on
flowers—living things with sex, pores, and susceptibilities.

In the like manner Virginia Woolf, using the tumult created
by high strong wind in the street as a symbol, suggests the state
of Ralph's mind at the time when he became conscious of his
love for Katharine:

The gusts, sweeping along the Strand, seemed at the same time to
blow a clear space across the sky in which stars appeared, and for a
short time the quick-speeding silver moon riding through clouds, as
if they were waves of water surging round her and over her .....
In the country fields all the wreckage of winter was being dispersed;
the dead leaves, the withered bracken, the dry and discoloured
grass, but no bud would be broken, nor would the new stalks that
showed above the earth take any harm, and perhaps to-morrow a
line of blue or yellow would show through a slit in their green.
                                                     (p. 416)

The clouds being swept away, and the wreckage of winter being
dispersed, suggest the removal of the uncertainties and illusions
of Ralph by his becoming conscious that he loves Katharine.
The unbroken buds and the newly sprouted stalks, which
would shortly show a line of blue or yellow through a slit in
their green, symbolize his secret hopes of happiness with
Katharine.

Similarly when Cassandra, William, Ralph, and Katharine,
arrive at Hampton Court, and walk up and down four abreast,
Cassandra feels blissful. 'The fresh air of spring, the sky washed
of clouds and already shedding warmth from its blue', 'the
stillness, the brightness, the air of expectancy which lay upon
the orderly beauty of the grass walks', 'the quivering stillness
of the butterfly on the half-opened flower', and 'the silent

grazing of the deer in the sun', all become symbols of the bliss and radiant happiness that Cassandra was feeling at that time (pp. 486–8).

Virginia Woolf also uses certain characters symbolically. Yet at the same time they do not cease to be themselves, for they are not meant to be allegorical or types equated to one quality or passion like the characters in morality plays or *The Pilgrim's Progress*. Her characters are mostly 'round' ones. She shows their different facets both from inside through their interior monologues, and from outside through the comments and reactions of other characters. It is only when by stressing their particular traits she suggests through them a certain state of mind, a particular aspect of an individual or society, or some passion or idea, that they attain symbolic value. Mr. and Mrs. Ambrose in *The Voyage Out*, Mr. and Mrs. Hilbery in *Night and Day*, and Mr. and Mrs. Ramsay in *To the Lighthouse*, are used to suggest intellect and intuition. She modelled these characters on her father and mother. Their recurring appearance in her novels she has explained thus:

I used to think of him and mother daily; but writing the *Lighthouse* laid them in my mind.   (*Diary*, p. 138)

Helen Ambrose in *The Voyage Out* has 'largeness and simplicity' (p. 157). She has understanding and sympathy. She can intuitively understand people. She helps them in their difficulties. She is able to understand Hirst in spite of his peculiar nature and she can be friendly with him when Rachel could not. She understands her husband, also, and is able to pacify him by tidying his room and making his chair more comfortable on board ship. But Mrs. Hilbery in *Night and Day* is an improvement on Helen. Her character has been delineated with greater care to suggest more aspects of intuition. She has a 'fine natural insight which saw deep whenever it saw at all' (p. 39). She is able to judge Denham by one long penetrating look, when she finds him studying Byron with Katharine in the dining-room (pp. 450–1). It is she again who through her intuitive insight is able to understand and straighten out the tangle between the two couples which had completely puzzled her husband. Without Mr. Hilbery telling her anything she knows all about it (p. 508). She is able to judge Denham correctly when he meets her in the shop. She seems to draw her conclusions by looking at her daughter instead of by discussing matters with her (p. 510). Above all, like all intuitive persons, she has vision and the power to believe (p. 148).

In the same way Mr. Ambrose and Mr. Hilbery, like Mr. Ramsay, represent intellect. Whereas Mr. Ambrose edits Pindar, Mr. Hilbery edits his reviews, or, placing together documents, tries to prove that Shelley wrote 'of' instead of 'and', or that the inn in which Byron had slept was called the 'Nag's Head' and not the 'Turkish Knight', or that the christian name of Keats's uncle had been John rather than Richard, for he knew more minute details about these poets than any man in England (p. 108). But when Katharine goes to talk to him about the affairs of Cyril, he is irritated and replies to her sharply, and with unwonted decision and authority (p. 110). Unlike his wife, who, being sympathetic, brings together Katharine and Denham, and Cassandra and Rodney, Mr. Hilbery is most unsympathetic and separates them all. He dispatches Cassandra to catch the eleven thirty on Monday morning (p. 506). He forbids Rodney the house, and asks Denham to make himself scarce (p. 503). Thus, being interested more in knowing whether Shelley wrote 'of' or 'and' than in knowing human nature Mr. Hilbery, like Professor Hobkin in 'A Society', and Professors Huxtable, Sopwith, and Cowan in *Jacob's Room*, becomes a caricature of dry intellection.

Mr. Pepper and Hirst in *The Voyage Out* also symbolize intellect. Out of these two Virginia Woolf seems to be more considerate towards Hirst who, perhaps, like Neville in *The Waves*, is modelled after Lytton Strachey. He, with his scissor-sharp intellect, is unaesthetic. He cannot understand music and dance. He knows the anatomy of the waltz without having imbibed any of its spirit (p. 178). Engrossed in taking 'serious things very seriously' (p. 183), the intellectuals in her novels are blind to 'the silly things' that people say when they are in love, on which, as Mrs. Hilbery says in *Night and Day*, life is built, and which are 'the only truth' (p. 324). Being unable to understand tenderness, or to care for the feelings of others, they are brusque and hurtful. In the hotel, when Hirst cannot dance properly, he and Rachel stagger to a seat in the corner of the room. After a long silence, he starts questioning her about her education. On Rachel's telling him that she had not read many classics, he advises her to read Gibbon.

'You must begin to-morrow. I shall send you my copy. What I want to know is—' he looked at her critically. 'You see, the problem is, can one really talk to you? Have you got a mind, or are you like the rest of your sex? You seem to me absurdly young compared with men of your age.'   (*The Voyage Out*, p. 180)

He, like Tansley in *To the Lighthouse*, who offensively tells Lily that 'women can't paint, women can't write' (p. 78), insolently asks Rachel whether she has a mind. His insolence is the outcome of his conceit that he is 'one of the three' most distinguished men of England.

The intellectuals in Virginia Woolf's novels can be divided into three classes: Mr. Ramsay in *To the Lighthouse*, Mr. Ambrose in *The Voyage Out*, and Mr. Hilbery in *Night and Day*, who, in spite of being brusque and hurtful, command her respect; Mr. Hirst in *The Voyage Out*, Rodney in *Night and Day* and Neville in *The Waves*, who fail to command her respect but have her admiration; Professor Hobkin in 'A Society', the Professors in *Jacob's Room*, Charles Tansley in *To the Lighthouse*, and Pepper in *The Voyage Out*, who get nothing but derision and ridicule. Out of all these, Mr. Pepper is the only intellectual in her novels with whom, as with Kilman and Sir William Bradshaw in *Mrs. Dalloway*, Virginia Woolf gets emotionally involved in the manner of D. H. Lawrence. She is not only unsympathetic, but mockingly harsh. Like her father, Sir Leslie Stephen,[1] she uses bird and beast imagery when making disparaging descriptions. Mr. Pepper, the 'Little man' with 'sinister conciseness', is a 'vivacious and malicious old ape', 'a fossilised fish', an 'ill-conditioned fox-terrier', 'a cormorant' and a 'cow'.[2]

The Dalloways, too, in *The Voyage Out* are used symbolically to suggest the modern sophisticated society. Regarding her impressions about the people on board the *Euphrosyne*, Mrs. Dalloway writes,

[1] In 'Leslie Stephen', *The Captain's Death Bed*, p. 68 she mentions how her father would draw 'owls and donkeys, as if to illustrate the "Oh you ass" or "Conceited dunce" ' which he wrote in the margins of his books.

[2] *The Voyage Out*, pp. 8, 9, 11, 13, 52 and 99.

The worst of it is, these people—a man and his wife and a niece—
might have been, one feels, just like everybody else, if they hadn't
got swallowed up by Oxford or Cambridge, or some such place, and
been made cranks of. The man's really delightful (if he'd cut his
nails), and the woman has quite a fine face, only she dresses, of
course, in a potato sack, and wears her hair like a Liberty shop-
girl's. They talk about art, and think us such poops for dressing in
the evening. However, I can't help that; I'd rather die than come
in to dinner without changing—wouldn't you? It matters ever so
much more than the soup. (It's odd how things like that *do* matter
so much more than what's generally supposed to matter. I'd rather
have my head cut off than wear flannel next the skin.)   (p. 51)

Mrs. Dalloway, who would rather die than come in to dinner
without changing, and who would have her head cut off rather
than wear flannel next to her skin, like Sophia who criticizes
her visitor merely because she had 'no gloves',[1] and like the
characters in Galsworthy who worried what their servants
would think about their walking down Baker Street without
gloves,[2] becomes, in contrast to the Ambroses, a symbol
of conventionality, outer snobbish vulgarity and inner spiritual
bankruptcy.

   Similarly Mrs. Milvain in *Night and Day* who 'beheld herself
the champion of married love in its purity and supremacy'
(p. 433), and who always comes to her brother's house to
discuss other people's behaviour—Cyril's misdemeanour,
Cassandra's lack of propriety (p. 429)—becomes a symbol of
prudish notions about love and marriage. It is the Victorian
prudery of Mrs. Milvain, and the docility in marriage of Lady
Otway, who pretended 'to like emeralds when she preferred
diamonds' (p. 225), that Mrs. Hilbery intuitively, and Ralph
and Katherine intellectually, are up against in *Night and Day*.

   In addition to using character symbolically to represent some
quality or an abstract idea, Virginia Woolf uses it in a subtler
way to evoke a state of mind. When Ralph does not find Rodney
at home, he comes and sits on a seat on the Embankment.

One of the regular occupants of those seats, an elderly man who had
drunk himself, probably, out of work and lodging, drifted up,
begged a match, and sat down beside him. It was a windy night, he

---

[1] Arnold Bennett, *The Old Wives' Tale*, London, 1927, p. 7.
[2] *The Times Literary Supplement*, 30 August 1917, p. 415.

said; times were hard; some long story of bad luck and injustice
followed ..... The ancient story of failure, ill-luck, undeserved disaster, went down the wind, disconnected syllables flying past
Ralph's ears ..... dying down at last into a grumble of resignation,
which seemed to represent a final lapse into the accustomed despair.

(p. 417)

The elderly man out of work and lodging, an embodiment of
failure, ill-luck and undeserved disaster, becomes a symbol of
Ralph's deep lying fear that after six months, when the marriage
between Rodney and Katharine would take place, for him
there would be 'the silence of the grave, the isolation of the
insane, the exile of the damned' (pp. 407–8). But he does not
want to be the unlucky, the unhappy one. Even though at the
moment he thinks that he is like the flying body of a lost bird
dashing against the glass, he feels that he is a lighthouse, too,
steadfast and brilliant, and that there is no cause to despair.
Hoping that something is going to happen, he gets up and starts
walking towards Katharine's house, and becomes 'full of
pleasure and expectancy'. When after tramping 'a beat up and
down the pavement before the Hilberys' gate' (p. 419), Ralph
meets Rodney coming out of Katharine's house, and finds that
Rodney is unhappy because of Katharine's laughter, he feels
secure. On knowing that Katharine does not love Rodney, and
that there is no likelihood of Rodney's marrying her, he feels
happy, and sees Rodney instead 'as one of the lost birds dashed
senseless against the glass; one of the flying bodies of which
the air was full' (p. 422).

To suggest the mental states of her characters, Virginia
Woolf also uses action and incident symbolically. At the dance
arranged to celebrate the engagement of Susan, Hirst tries to
dance with Rachel who, because of a good ear for rhythm,
could dance well.

A single turn proved to them that their methods were incompatible;
instead of fitting into each other their bones seemed to jut out in
angles making smooth turning an impossibility, and cutting, moreover, into the circular progress of the other dancers.

(*The Voyage Out*, pp. 178–9)

Their not being able to dance together becomes symbolic
of their minds not being in harmony with each other, and
of their not being meant for each other.

After the dance is over Hirst and Hewet walk with Rachel and Helen up to the Villa. There they sit down for a while near the gate, and Rachel occupies herself 'in collecting one grey stone after another and building them into a little cairn'. This collecting of stones and building them up into a cairn 'quietly and carefully' symbolizes the thinking out of her thoughts, and the building up of a pattern of life for herself, especially after having undergone the experience at the dance where she was 'very happy', and where she had changed her 'view of life completely' (p. 191). She was no longer a timid girl with her wits scattered all over the place. On the other hand, she had become possessed of all her faculties. Now none 'of these people possessed any power to frighten her out here in the dawn, and she felt perfectly familiar even with Mr. Hirst' (p. 198).

In *Night and Day*, too, there are certain actions that Virginia Woolf uses as symbols. When Ralph and Mary go out walking to Lincoln, he, 'filled with a sense of the actual presence of Katharine', leans against a tree and says aloud, 'Katharine, Katharine'. Walking away slowly from him, Mary tears 'a long spray of ivy from the trees' (p. 235). This tearing away of ivy is symbolic of the feelings of Mary who thinks that she must tear herself away from Ralph—her tree—because he is in love with Katharine. But as they start walking again, and discussing Denham's prospect of buying a cottage and writing a book,

She wound her ivy spray round her ash-plant, and for the first time for many days, when alone with Ralph, set no spies on her motives, sayings, and feelings, but surrendered herself to complete happiness.   (p. 237)

The winding of the ivy round her stick becomes suggestive of her feeling that she yet can cling to Ralph. But, sitting in the inn at Lincoln, she becomes certain that Ralph is in love with Katharine. On their preparing to go back,

Ralph handed her coat and her stick. She took them, fastened the coat securely, grasped the stick firmly. The ivy spray was still twisted about the handle; this one sacrifice, she thought, she might make to sentimentality and personality, and she picked two leaves from the ivy and put them in her pocket before she dis-encumbered her stick of the rest of it. She grasped the stick in the middle, and settled her fur cap closely upon her head, as if she must be in trim for a long and stormy walk.   (p. 243–4)

The throwing away of the ivy after fastening the coat securely, and grasping the stick firmly, symbolize her decision and determination not to cling to Ralph as he did not belong to her any more. Consequently she refuses to marry him when, later, on their journey back home, he proposes to her (p. 261).

Herself 'a tireless solitary walker about London',[1] Virginia Woolf employs the act of walking symbolically. When Rachel feels an exultation, and has a suspicion that she is falling in love, her unconsciously 'walking faster and faster' becomes suggestive of her inner excitement. Hewet, too, when he sees Hirst slip into a chair by Rachel's side, resorts to walking 'fast in spite of the heat of the sun'. The speed of his walk varies according to the prevalent mood of the moment. He walks fast as long as he is tormented. As soon as he starts speaking about his love of her, his pace slackens. He stays and leans against a tree, when he visualizes her 'face distinctly, the grey eyes, the hair, the mouth; the face that could look so many things—'. And no sooner does he open his arms wide in exultation 'as if to hold her and the world in one embrace' than he drops to the ground and sits absorbed in the thought of her (pp. 293–8).

Ralph and Katharine, too, in *Night and Day* are found walking, tramping, or running according to their state of mind. When mentally perturbed, Ralph walks 'up the street at a great pace, cutting the air with his walking-stick' (p. 16), or strides 'with extreme swiftness' along the Embankment (p. 161), or runs up the stairs 'two steps at a time' (p. 410), or tramps a beat up and down (p. 419). Similarly Katharine's walking up and down, her driving quickly, hastening to and from Lincoln's Inn, and speeding in a cab, reflect the agitated states of her mind (pp. 202, 375, 466, and 478).

Whenever characters in *The Voyage Out* and *Night and Day* have to express an idea which they cannot convey adequately in a direct statement, they try to evoke it by making use of symbols. In *The Voyage Out* Evelyn and Hewet, when discussing men, come to a point where Hewet cannot explain clearly what exactly he means by 'People are—nothing more'.

[1] Elizabeth Bowen, *Collected Impressions*, London, 1950, p. 81.

On Evelyn's looking puzzled, Hewet tries to explain himself. He says, 'We don't care for people because of their qualities ..... It's just them that we care for.' On feeling that he has not been able to make himself understood, he strikes a match, and pointing to the flame repeats, 'just that' (p. 227). Evelyn sees his meaning in a flash. The flame becomes a symbol of the spirit of man, and not his body and its attributes.

In the same way Katharine in *Night and Day* makes use of flames and fires to explain her idea about Ralph. 'What a fire', she thinks on looking towards Ralph.

She thought of him blazing splendidly in the night, yet so obscure that to hold his arm, as she held it, was only to touch the opaque substance surrounding the flame that roared upward.   (p. 533)

Noticing her dreaminess when he asks her to tell him everything from the beginning, she says that she is a person who can't tell things, and that, if she tries, she will say something ridiculous— something about flames and fires (p. 534). Flames and fires, like the sparks issuing from Shelley's 'Burning Fountain', thus symbolize the spirit, the essential in man.

When Ralph Denham instead of concentrating on the last Will and Testament of the late John Leake of Dublin saw through its pages a certain drawing-room in Cheyne Walk, then

By degrees, a pulse or stress began to beat at regular intervals in his mind, heaping his thoughts into waves to which words fitted themselves, and without much consciousness of what he was doing, he began to write on a sheet of draft paper what had the appearance of a poem lacking several words in each line. Not many lines had been set down, however before, he ..... tore the paper into many separate pieces .....

It was a difficult matter to put into words; ..... In idleness and because he could do nothing further with words, he began to draw little figures in the blank spaces, heads meant to resemble her head, blots fringed with flames meant to represent—perhaps the entire universe.   (pp. 514–16)

When Ralph Denham, feeling like T. S. Eliot that

> Words strain
> Crack and sometimes break, under the burden
> Under the tension, slip, slide, perish,

cannot express the 'confused and emotional' moment in words, he tries to symbolize it by drawing a central blot surrounded by a circumference of smudges, which convey to him 'not only Katharine herself but all those states of mind which had clustered round her since he saw her pouring out tea on a Sunday afternoon' (p. 522).

Trees, rivers, and houses, too, Virginia Woolf employs symbolically. In *The Voyage Out* when Rachel goes out with 'Gibbon's *History of the Roman Empire*', and Balzac's *La Cousine Bette*, she sees a tree.

> It was an ordinary tree, but to her it appeared so strange that it might have been the only tree in the world. Dark was the trunk in the middle, and the branches sprang here and there, leaving jagged intervals of light between them as distinctly as if it had but that second risen from the ground. (pp. 204-5)

In *Night and Day* when they alight from the carriage and walk along the cart-track, William talks to Katharine about his love for her, and wants to know whether she loves him. She wants to tell him the truth—that it was in a misty state of mind that she accepted him, and that in fact she does not love him. She summons her courage and, fixing her eyes on a 'lightning-splintered tree', professes the truth. The lightning-splintered tree becomes for her a symbol of the life that would be hers if she married William without having any love for him.

Whenever the characters in these two novels muse about life, especially married life, they think of, or peer down into, a river. In *The Voyage Out* the second expedition sails up a river. It is on this expedition that Rachel and Hewet fall in love, and decide to get married, to voyage out on the river of life. Mrs. Hilbery, too, in *Night and Day*, recalls a similar experience of going out on a voyage up a river when she wants to explain to Katharine what her feelings were when she decided to get married.

> 'We were in a little boat going out to a ship at night,' she began. 'The sun had set and the moon was rising over our heads. There were lovely silver lights upon the waves and three green lights upon the steamer in the middle of the bay. Your father's head looked so grand against the mast. It was life, it was death. The great sea was round us. It was the voyage for ever and ever. (pp. 511-12)

After having talked about marriage with Helen, when Rachel and Hewet in *The Voyage Out* rise and hang over the rail, they see 'beneath them the smooth black water' slipping away 'very fast and silently' (p. 353). Similarly in *Night and Day*, when the tangle between the two pairs has been smoothed out by Mrs. Hilbery in her own intuitive way, Katharine and Ralph go out for a walk. On their way back home

Pausing, they looked down into the river which bore its dark tide of waters, endlessly moving, beneath them.   (p. 538)

The flowing river thus becomes a symbol of life and marriage which are like a 'voyage for ever and ever'.

As the trees and rivers signify growing and flowing life, so buildings symbolize various systems and modes of life. 'The hotel' and 'the villa' in *The Voyage Out* do not seem to represent 'individual world' and 'social world', as James Hafley thinks that they do.[1] On carefully studying the novel, it appears that Virginia Woolf was not suggesting the theme of the individual as against the social, nor was she portraying the residents of the villa as individualistic people. But they do represent, as Virginia Woolf herself writes, 'two separate systems of life'. The hotel had 'a slightly inhuman atmosphere' but to escape to the house was a 'source of genuine pleasure' (p. 268). In the same way Rachel's house at Richmond which, according to her own description of it is 'rather a nice house ..... except that it's a little dingy—dull', with a drawing-room 'without definite character, being neither typically and openly hideous, nor strenuously artistic, nor really comfortable'— this house, with its four meals, its punctuality, and servants on the stair at half past ten, becomes a symbol of the Victorian conventional type of life that was imposed on the daughters of the house, and which, Virginia Woolf the feminist thinks, left the daughter inexperienced, raw and unlicked even at the age of twenty-four (p. 255).

Besides these, Virginia Woolf has symbolically employed other images. When Evelyn met Perrott in the garden, and Perrott asked her to marry him

[1] *The Glass Roof—Virginia Woolf as Novelist*, University of California Press, 1954, p. 16.

she felt less for him than she had ever felt before.

'Let's sit down and talk it over,' she said rather unsteadily.

Mr. Perrott followed her to a curved green seat under a tree. They looked at the fountain in front of them, which had long ceased to play.   (p. 446)

The fountain without any water that had long ceased to play not only becomes a symbol of the dry frozen feelings of Evelyn, but also becomes a symbol of their friendship which had turned out to be as useless as the dry fountain.

Just as the dry fountain symbolizes the condition of Evelyn's heart, so Katharine's passion for mathematics and astronomy signifies her mental make-up and personality. Katharine prefers to 'work at mathematics' which, she thought, were directly opposed to literature. She wants 'to know about the stars', and 'to study mathematics and the science of astronomy', 'to work out something in figures—something that hasn't got to do with human beings'. Therefore, 'A plus B minus C equals $x\,y\,z$' with its impersonality of figures and the orderliness of stars becomes a symbol of her lack of love and faith, hence her loneliness, and of her disposition—'Ordering meals, directing servants, paying bills, and so contriving that every clock ticked more or less accurately in time .....' which, according to Mrs. Hilbery, is 'poetry the wrong side out'. When Mrs. Hilbery, therefore, tells Denham, 'I'm so glad you've made Katharine read poetry, Mr. Denham! ..... and feel poetry, and look poetry!', it becomes symbolic of Katharine's overcoming her dry impersonality of figures, and of her falling in love.[1]

When the characters in the novels are in a hypersensitive state of mind, the ordinary things of the everyday world gain symbolic significance and show them a glimpse of reality or evoke visions in them. The day Rachel went to the hotel to attend chapel, she spent some time talking first to Evelyn, and then to Miss Allan. Leaving Miss Allan, when she found Mrs. Paley blocking up the passage

She walked quickly and blindly in the opposite direction, and found herself at the end of a *cul de sac*. There was a window, and a table and a chair in the window, and upon the table stood a rusty inkstand, an ash-tray, an old copy of a French newspaper, and a pen with a broken nib. ..... It had been miserable from start to finish; first the service

[1] *Night and Day*, pp. 40, 203, 254, 203, 511, 38, 517.

in the chapel; then luncheon; then Evelyn; then Miss Allan; then old Mrs. Paley blocking up the passage ..... She had now reached one of those eminences, the result of some crisis, from which the world is finally displayed in its true proportions. She disliked the look of it immensely—churches, politicians, misfits, and huge impostures—men like Mr. Dalloway, men like Mr. Bax, Evelyn and her chatter, Mrs. Paley blocking up the passage ..... She considered the rusty inkstand, the pen, the ash-tray and the old French newspaper. These small and worthless objects seemed to her to represent human lives.   (*The Voyage Out*, pp. 314–16)

As the rusty inkstand, the old newspaper, and the pen with a broken nib become symbolic to Rachel of the smallness and worthlessness of human life, so the little figures of the small senseless beasts, whose cries rang high and low from tree-trunk to tree-top, making Helen

acutely conscious of the little limbs, the thin veins, the delicate flesh of men and women, which breaks so easily and lets the life escape compared with these great trees and deep waters   (pp. 349–50)

become to her, like the bubbles for Rickie in E. M. Forster's *The Longest Journey*,[1] symbolic of the transitoriness of human life.

[1] London, 1924, p. 69.

CHAPTER THREE

Jacob's Room

I<small>T</small> appears that while Virginia Woolf was writing *Night and Day*, which she completed in March 1919, she had become conscious of a certain type of constraint imposed by the necessity of there being a formal design to a novel. Explaining this later in her essay on 'Modern Fiction', she says:

The writer seems constrained, not by his own free will but by some powerful and unscrupulous tyrant who has him in thrall, to provide a plot, to provide comedy, tragedy, love interest, and an air of probability embalming the whole so impeccable that if all his figures were to come to life they would find themselves dressed down to the last button of their coats in the fashion of the hour.

(*The Common Reader*, First Series, p. 188)

She seems to have come to the conclusion that to obey this 'unscrupulous tyrant' is to cease to portray one's vision of life, and that a novelist who tries to give an air of probability is in danger of becoming dependent on facts, and unable to achieve 'a truth of insight which is far rarer and more enduring than the truth of fact'.[1] Therefore, as early as 1917, emboldened, perhaps, by the publication of *Portrait of the Artist as a Young Man* by James Joyce, and of *Pointed Roofs* by Dorothy Richardson, Virginia Woolf, too, tried to find a method of portraying her vision of life by writing 'The Mark on the Wall'. The style of 'The Mark on the Wall', resembles more the style of the cemetery scene in *Ulysses*, which James Joyce wrote in 1919, but she still felt constricted. She was seeking a new form which would give her a 'looseness and lightness'[2] and would come nearer to portraying her vision of what life is with its 'brilliancy, its sordidity, its incoherence, its sudden lightning flashes of significance'.[3] Yet she feared a more powerful, tyrant—'the damned

---

[1] 'Defoe', *The Common Reader*, First Series, p. 130. This essay first appeared in *The Times Literary Supplement* on 24 April 1919.   [2] *Diary*, p. 23.
[3] 'Modern Fiction', *The Common Reader*, First Series, p. 191.

egotistical self',[1] which, she felt, had ruined Joyce and Richardson
by being 'narrowing and restricting'. To free herself from this
she was trying different methods in *Kew Gardens*, 1919, *Solid
Objections*, 1920, *Unwritten Novel*, 1920, and *Monday or Tuesday*,
1921, and had mused over what modern fiction should be like
in her two critical essays on 'Modern Fiction', and 'Defoe',
both written in 1919. She had judged the merits and shortcomings of Joyce and of Richardson, as recorded in her diary
and in her unsigned review of *The Tunnel*,[2] and she was becoming confident that she, like Laurence Sterne in *Tristram Shandy*,
could tell a story in her own way. Meanwhile she had started
to write *Jacob's Room* in 1920. This, her first novel of idea, in
keeping with her advice written to Lytton Strachey in 1908
that 'Plots don't matter', has neither a conventional plot nor
any traditional characterization. As a result of this it appeared
to Deborah Newton to be 'a series of exquisite essays',[3] and
to Herbert J. Muller a 'fragmentary disconnected mental experience'.[4] To E. M. Forster, on the other hand, the coherence
of the book seems to be 'more amazing than its beauty'.[5]
The various scenes and incidents, and the different episodes,
are all threaded around the young personality of Jacob, and
the incidents, unlike those in *Mrs. Dalloway* where she tunnels into
the past, are chronologically narrated. In contrast with Bennett,
Wells, and Galsworthy who, she says in 'Modern Fiction',
are concerned 'not with the spirit but with the body', Virginia
Woolf in *Jacob's Room* is not concerned with actions or dramatic
scenes, but with dreams and visions of life and personality.
Like the Russian writers, whom she was studying and translat-
ing during this period, she strives to give us an insight into the
working of the minds of her characters, and endeavours to
externalize their emotional states. The human soul becomes,
as she observes it to be in Russian fiction, the chief character in
her novel.[6] Besides portraying the human soul and personality,
Virginia Woolf tries to suggest her ideas about modern civilization and the loneliness of man.

[1] *Diary*, p. 23.
[2] *The Times Literary Supplement*, 13 February 1919, p. 81.
[3] *Virginia Woolf*, Melbourne University Press, 1946, p. 31.
[4] *Modern Fiction*, London, 1937, p. 61.
[5] *Abinger Harvest*, London, 1940, p. 107.
[6] 'The Russian Point of View', *The Common Reader*, First Series, p. 225.

Deeply agitated by the devastations of the first world war, when Leonard Woolf was expressing his reactions in *After the Deluge*, and when G. L. Dickinson and others were writing about war, its nature, causes and cure, Virginia Woolf, too, in her own artistic way, was trying to suggest its horrors and to point out its causes. *Jacob's Room*, therefore, is perhaps the saddest of her novels, even more sad than *The Voyage Out* in which Rachel dies in the prime of her life shortly after becoming conscious of the beauties and pleasures of life. Her death is not depressing, because it does not in the least convey a sense of frustration, or of life wantonly destroyed, indeed it explains life and reality. It is through Rachel's death that Terence realizes union and perfect happiness. But Jacob's death is like that of flies killed by wanton boys. It portrays the gnawing fear which one of the characters in 'A Society', (which Virginia Woolf wrote during that time), on hearing the cries of 'War, war, war. Declaration of war', expresses about the horror of bearing children to see them killed.[1] That Virginia Woolf felt acutely the frustrating effects of war is evident from the entries in her diary. On 25 October 1920 she wrote:

Why is life so tragic; so like a little strip of pavement over an abyss. I look down; I feel giddy; I wonder how I am ever to walk to the end.

Then she questions herself why she feels like that. She thinks of different things that could be the cause of it: her having no children; living away from friends; failing to write well; spending too much on food; pocket money not allowing much. She rejects them all and comes to the conclusion that

it's life itself, I think sometimes, for us in our generation so tragic— no newspaper placard without its shriek of agony from someone. McSwiney this afternoon and violence in Ireland; or it'll be the strike. Unhappiness is everywhere; just beyond the door; or stupidity, which is worse.

Writing on 13 August 1921 about Lady Carlisle's death, she says,

Such a stock of hope and gifts she set out with, and lost everything (so they say) and died of sleepy sickness, her 5 sons dead before her and the war crushing her hope for humanity.

[1] *Monday or Tuesday*, London, 1921, p. 32.

Even though the events in the first chapter of *Jacob's Room* happen before Jacob goes up to Cambridge in 1906, they yet reflect the contemporary events and feelings hinted above, and the novel opens on a note of fear and insecurity. Betty Flanders is a widow, and like all widows, as Mrs. Jarvis, the Rector's wife thinks, she is a 'lonely, unprotected, poor' creature who has lost the fortress of marriage, and is burdened with the upbringing of her three sons (p. 6).

Slowly welling from the point of her gold nib, pale blue ink dissolved the full stop; for there her pen stuck; her eyes fixed, and tears slowly filled them. The entire bay quivered; the lighthouse wobbled; and she had the illusion that the mast of Mr. Connor's little yacht was bending like a wax candle in the sun.   (p.5)

This distortion which the scene undergoes when the eyes fill with tears, becomes symbolic of the distortion one experiences under the stress of fear and insecurity. To a widow like Betty Flanders all the world appears to have gone crooked to the point of breaking asunder. She is, therefore, uncomfortably apprehensive, and, abruptly finishing her letter to Captain Barfoot, she sets out in search of Jacob who has wandered away on the beach.

This sense of dread and fright that Mrs. Flanders feels, runs through the first section of *Jacob's Room*. At the very instant that Betty Flanders feels uneasy regarding the safety of Jacob, Charles Steele, who has been trying to include her in his land-scape painting, experiences another type of horror. He is afraid that Betty would get up and start moving in search of her son, and thus spoil his picture. He tries to hurry, but at the very moment as he looks up he sees 'to his horror a cloud over the bay' (p. 7).

Simultaneously we are given a peep into the frightened mind of yet another character. While playing on the beach, Jacob sees a man and woman 'stretched motionless, with their heads on pocket-handkerchiefs, side by side, within a few feet of the sea'. To his young frightened mind they look to be 'enormous'. He is terrified, and, seized with childish panic, he takes to his heels, sobbing.

This sense of fear that she lodges in the minds of these three characters Virginia Woolf heightens to the point of weirdness by

D

externalizing it in terms of outward scenes and atmosphere. When Archer shouts 'Ja—cob! Ja—cob!'

The voice had an extraordinary sadness. Pure from all body, pure from all passion, going out into the world, solitary, unanswered, breaking against rocks—so it sounded.

The solitary, unanswered, breaking against rocks sound with its extraordinary sadness evokes a peculiar kind of uneasiness in the mind of the reader. This effect she amplifies by using images of instability and weakness.

But there, on the very top, is a hollow full of water, with a sandy bottom; with a blob of jelly stuck to the side, and some mussels. A fish darts across. The fringe of yellow-brown seaweed flutters, and out pushes an opal-shelled crab ..... and begins its journey on weakly legs on the sandy bottom.   (p. 7)

The hollow full of water, the sandy bottom, and the weakly legged crab, suggesting instability and weakness, add to the sense of Mrs. Flanders' helplessness which Virginia Woolf is trying to convey.

In contradistinction to the unsteady blob of jelly and the weakly legged crab, Virginia Woolf describes a rising storm. It not only externalizes 'the buried discomfort' that lay 'in the depths' of Betty's mind, but also heightens the already accumulating sense of fear.

..... and the wind rising, she took out her bonnet-pin, looked at the sea, and stuck it in afresh. The wind was rising. The waves showed that uneasiness, like something alive, restive, expecting the whip, of waves before a storm. The fishing-boats were leaning to the water's brim. A pale yellow light shot across the purple sea; and shut. The lighthouse was lit ..... The sun blazed in their faces and gilded the great blackberries trembling out from the hedge which Archer tried to strip as they passed.

'Don't lag boys. You've got nothing to change into,' said Betty, pulling them along, and looking with uneasy emotion at the earth displayed so luridly, with sudden sparks of light from greenhouses in gardens, with a sort of yellow and black mutability, against this blazing sunset, this astonishing agitation and vitality of colour, which stirred Betty Flanders and made her think of responsibility and danger.   (p. 9)

The rising wind, the uneasiness of the restive waves, and the astonishing agitation and vitality of colour, evoke an eerie sense as if something calamitous is going to happen. She further enhances this sense by creating as restive an atmosphere as this agitated landscape. The hurricane out at sea, and the 'straight dashes of rain across the window' make the lodging-house seem to be full of 'gurgling and rushing; the cistern overflowing; water bubbling and squeaking and running along the pipes and streaming down the windows' (p. 10). They keep Archer from sleep. The sights outside the house, also, are as frightening as the sounds inside it. Outside

..... the wind was tearing across the coast, hurling itself at the hills, and leaping, in sudden gusts, on top of its own back ..... And rolling dark waves before it, it raced over the Atlantic, jerking the stars above the ships this way and that. (pp. 11–12)

And when Mr. Pearce, the landlord, extinguished the lamp

The garden went out. It was but a dark patch ..... Lying on one's back one would have seen nothing but muddle and confusion—clouds turning and turning, and something yellow-tinted and sulphurous in the darkness.

In that sinister darkness 'Every blade of grass was bent by rain', and 'the aster was beaten to the earth', and in the half-full bucket the opal-shelled crab was trying with its weakly legs to climb the steep side, trying again and falling back, and trying again and again' (p. 12). The weakly legged crab circling round and round the bottom of the bucket unable to climb out, and the aster beaten to the earth, become symbolic of the helplessness of Betty Flanders. Similarly the tearing, hurling, leaping wind, the muddled clouds turning and turning, and something yellow-tinted and sulphurous, symbolize the insecure fearful world around her.

Thus by using evocative images, sights, and sounds, Virginia Woolf suggests symbolically the complexity of fear, insecurity, and helplessness which was overshadowing the mind of Mrs. Flanders, and which she could not convey effectively otherwise.

In the same way, by employing the geese symbol Virginia Woolf gives us an insight into the working of Betty's mind.

When Betty took Mr. Floyd's letter from the hall, and, thinking it to be about the boys, went into the kitchen to read it,
she found after all that it had nothing to do with them. She
came to the word 'love' and, leaving the kitchen,

went into the garden and read, leaning against the walnut tree
to steady herself. Up and down went her breast. Seabrook came so
vividly before her. She shook her head and was looking through her
tears at the little shifting leaves against the yellow sky when three
geese, half-running, half-flying, scuttled across the lawn with
Johnny behind them, brandishing a stick.

Mrs. Flanders flushed with anger.

'How many times have I told you?' she cried, and seized him and
snatched his stick away from him.

'But they'd escaped!' he cried, struggling to get free.

'You're a very naughty boy. If I've told you once, I've told you a
thousand times. I won't *have* you chasing the geese!' she said, and
crumpling Mr. Floyd's letter in her hand, she held Johnny fast and
herded the geese back into the orchard.

'How could I think of marriage!' she said to herself bitterly, as
she fastened the gate with a piece of wire. She had always disliked
red hair in men, she thought, thinking of Mr. Floyd's appearance,
that night when the boys had gone to bed. And pushing her work-
box away, she drew the blotting-paper towards her, and read Mr.
Floyd's letter again, and her breast went up and down when she
came to the word 'love', but not so fast this time, for she saw Johnny
chasing the geese, and knew that it was impossible for her to marry
any one—let alone Mr. Floyd, who was so much younger than she
was, but what a nice man—and such a scholar too.   (pp. 18–19)

In a flash we see why she decided against marriage, and why,
in spite of her having flushed in anger, she held Johnny fast.
We intuitively understand that it is not because she disliked
red hair in men that she decided not to marry Mr. Floyd, but
because, having seen the three half-running, half-flying geese
being chased out, she got frightened, realizing that, were she to
marry, her second husband might chase out her three sons—
her three geese. Therefore, even though she was angry with
Johnny for chasing the geese, she unconsciously, perhaps, held
him fast in a protective maternal embrace shielding him thus
from an imaginary attack from an imaginary husband. This
apprehension of fear made her decide that 'it was impossible
for her to marry any one—let alone Mr. Floyd who was so

much younger than she was'. Thus by the apt use of the geese symbol, Virginia Woolf makes us comprehend immediately the intricate working of Betty's mind, and her unconscious reasoning and emotional reactions. This symbolic use of bird imagery is a definite improvement on her use of it in her first two novels, where she employs it, more in the manner of Henry James, in describing Mr. Pepper and some of the other people staying at the hotel in *The Voyage Out*, and in evoking certain characteristics in *Night and Day*.

We see another aspect of Virginia Woolf's symbolism in the way she telescopes the various traits of her protagonist's character into one suggestive symbol. Jacob Flanders,[1] was fond of serious study. Out of the three brothers he alone went up to a University. In his room at Cambridge were all the Elizabethans, Spinoza, *The Faerie Queene* the works of Dickens and 'The works of Jane Austen, too, in deference, perhaps, to some one else's standard' (p. 37). He reads *Phaedrus* late into the night, discusses Virgil and Lucretius with his friend, quotes Sophocles, recommends Marlowe and Fielding to Fanny; he is the only one with a book in his hand out of the multitudes seen from the steps of St. Paul's Cathedral, and he carries a book with him up to the Acropolis to read it there, for his love of learning did not cease with his education at Cambridge.[2] Jacob was also a great admirer of Greece and the Greek way of life. He not only left London and went to Greece, but, as he wrote to Bonamy, he intended to go there every year so long as he lived (p. 145). It was, therefore, partly due to this admiration that he fell for Florinda who, he thought, was 'free, venturesome, high-spirited' like all good women in the days of the Greeks (p. 75). The other prominent trait of Jacob's character was his obstinacy. He was the only one of Betty's sons who, as she rightly felt, never obeyed her (p. 21). All these traits of Jacob's character—love of learning, admiration for Greece, a rebellious nature, what Virginia Woolf calls Byronic male virtue, the effect he had on women, especially rather stupid or uneducated women unable to stand up to him, which

[1] One is tempted to conjecture that his surname comes from Moll Flanders, about whom V.W. was writing in 1919 only a short time before starting *Jacob's Room*.
[2] *Jacob's Room*, pp. 65, 74, 108, 121, 149.

Jacob is shown to have in abundance—all these she telescopes into one condensed symbol: his choosing, when asked by Mr. Floyd to take whatever he liked in his study to remember him by, 'the works of Byron in one volume' (p. 19).

Virginia Woolf also employs symbols whenever she has either to suggest the states of, or to give us an insight into, the minds of various characters in *Jacob's Room*. When Jacob leaves Cambridge, he goes out yachting with Timmy Durrant. This going out yachting, like Rachel's sailing out in *The Voyage Out*, becomes symbolic of his going out into life. At Durrant's he falls in love with Clara. He goes out gathering grapes with her. Mounted on a ladder

She looked semi-transparent, pale, wonderfully beautiful up there among the vine leaves and the yellow and purple bunches, the lights swimming over her in coloured islands. Geraniums and begonias stood in pots along planks; tomatoes climbed the walls .....

'It does seem absurd . . .' Clara began, 'going back to London . . .'

'Ridiculous,' said Jacob, firmly.

'Then . . .' said Clara, 'you must come next year, properly,' she said, snipping another vine leaf, rather at random.

'If . . . if . . .'

A child ran past the greenhouse shouting. Clara slowly descended the ladder with her basket of grapes.

'One bunch of white, and two of purple,' she said, and she placed two great leaves over them where they lay curled warm in the basket.

'I have enjoyed myself,' said Jacob, looking down the greenhouse.

'Yes it's been delightful,' she said vaguely.

'Oh, Miss Durrant,' he said, taking the basket of grapes; but she walked past him towards the door of the greenhouse.

'You are too good—too good,' she thought, thinking of Jacob, thinking that he must not say that he loved her. No, no, no.

The children were whirling past the door, throwing things high into the air.

'Little demons!' she cried. 'What have they got?' she asked Jacob.

'Onions, I think,' said Jacob. He looked at them without moving.

(pp. 60–61)

Like the Brontës, Meredith, and Hardy, Virginia Woolf places the young lovers against an appropriate background, in this case grape-laden vines and flowering plants, to symbolize their unexpressed desires, and vague, still unconscious, longing for children of their own. One bunch of white grapes and two of purple, lying curled warm in the basket, suggest an innocent babe and two hearts aflame with desire. Similarly while expressing their happiness—Jacob has enjoyed himself, and for Clara it has been delightful—the greenhouse, as Jacob looks at it and Clara goes towards it, becomes symbolic too. It is a symbol for nursery and hints at their desire for children. But this remains an unfulfilled dream. The prophetic vision that nothing will come out of it is symbolized by the children playing with onions which, when all their layers are removed yield nothing.

When Virginia Woolf wants to give us an insight into Jacob's state of mind at the time when he was cheated by Florinda, she makes use of nature symbols.

It was as if a stone were ground to dust; as if white sparks flew from a livid whetstone, which was his spine; as if the switchback railway, having swooped to the depths, fell, fell, fell. This was in his face.
Whether we know what was in his mind is another question.

(p. 93)

She has tried to describe something of his facial expression, but when it comes to describing the state of his mind, Virginia Woolf, feeling the inadequacy of direct statement, turns to symbolic suggestion.

..... He has turned to go ..... back to his rooms ..... The snow, which had been falling all night, lay at three o'clock in the afternoon over the fields and the hill. Clumps of withered grass stood out upon the hill-top; the furze bushes were black, and now and then a black shiver crossed the snow ..... The sky was sullen grey and the trees of black iron ..... Later there was a mournful cry . . . A motor car came along the road shoving the dark before it. . . . The dark shut down behind it. . . .
Spaces of complete immobility separated each of these movements. The land seemed to lie dead. (pp. 94, 97-98)

Thus employing symbols of snow, clumps of withered grass, a black shiver, the sullen sky, a mournful cry, and the land appearing to lie dead, Virginia Woolf evokes Jacob's state of mind—lost, cold, and emotionally dead.

Commenting on the books written by Wells, Bennett, and Galsworthy, Virginia Woolf in 'Modern Fiction' calls them 'materialists', and says that they write of unimportant things and spend immense skill and industry in making 'the trivial and the transitory appear the true and the enduring'. Again speaking about the modern literature in 'How it Strikes a Contemporary', she says,

Book after book leaves us with the same sense of promise unachieved, of intellectual poverty, of brilliance which has been snatched from life but not transmuted into literature.

(*The Common Reader*, First Series, p. 300)

Therefore Wells and Shaw, and the sixpenny weeklies—'written by pale men in muddy boots', the result of creaking and screeching 'of brains rinsed in cold water and wrung dry'—which Jacob sees at Mr. Plumer's house, standing for modern literature, as contrasted to 'Homer, Shakespeare, the Elizabethans' in Jacob's room, become a symbol of the triviality and intellectual poverty of Mr. Plumer's mind, and of Mrs. Plumer's shallow and tinselly outlook on life. Because Mr. Plumer, old Huxtable, Sopwith, and Cowan—the lights of Greek, Science, and Philosophy burning in Cambridge—like Professor Hobkin in 'A Society', seem not to be able to 'produce good people and good books',[1] the light burning over Cambridge 'is not simple, or pure, or wholly splendid'.[2]

Virginia Woolf seems to believe that modern civilization is an outward show and inward emptiness, a 'waste land' populated by 'hollow men'. As inner emptiness often breeds a morbid hankering after sensational excitement and sensual pleasures, life becomes restless. There is neither peace nor piety left. Consequently society becomes perverted, corrupt, and diseased. To emphasize these various aspects of modern civilization, she uses a condensed symbol: London. Like T. S. Eliot's

> Jerusalem Athens Alexandria
> Vienna London
> Unreal[3]

and like Baudelaire's Paris

> Fourmillante cité, cité pleine de rêves,
> Où le spectre en plein jour raccroche le passant!

[1] *Monday or Tuesday*, London, 1921, p. 21.
[2] *Jacob's Room*, pp. 33–34.   [3] 'The Waste Land'.

London, where Jacob goes after Cambridge, becomes a symbol of the futility and barrenness of modern civilization.

The blazing of the bonfire after 'two legs of a table', and 'a scattering of twigs and leaves' had been dropped on it, the wearing of 'conical white' and 'billycock' hats, and the singing and waltzing to the barrel organ music on Guy Fawkes' night when Jacob sat wreathed on a white and gilt chair, and Florinda 'got upon his knee and hid her face in his waistcoat', become symbolic of sensational excitement indulged in by 'taut' and 'intent faces' (pp. 73–74).

The incessantly moving multitudes of London, the innumerable overcoats that hang empty all day in the corridors but as the clock strikes six fill and jerk rapidly with angular forward motion along the pavement, and then dropping into darkness are conveyed this way and that (p. 65), and the hordes crossing the Waterloo Bridge, the moving carts, omnibuses, lorries, masons' vans, and motor cars, and the never ceasing stream of people passing from the Surrey side to the Strand, and from the Strand to the Surrey side, all suggest the restlessness of metropolitan life (pp. 112–13).

In *Jacob's Room* the sordid life of the metropolis is represented by Florinda, Laurette, Fanny, the arguing Jew and the woman, Mother Stuart, the confidante of Florinda, and Madame— the prostitutes and the bawdy matrons of London. Virginia Woolf, like Aphra Behn, T. S. Eliot, and Baudelaire, seems to be conscious of this aspect of city life also. Aphra Behn, as V. Sackville-West quotes her, says,

What a lewd world we live in! Oh London, London, how thou aboundest in iniquity! Thy young men are debauched, thy virgins deflowered, and thy matrons all turned bawds.[1]

Similarly Baudelaire is agonized on seeing the women of Paris. He laments,

> Et vous, femmes, hélas! pâles comme des cierges,
> Que ronge et que nourrit la débauche, et vous, vierges,
> Du vice maternel traînant l'hérédité
> Et toutes les hideurs de la fécondité!

Virginia Woolf in *Jacob's Room*, therefore, shows Jacob, on

[1] *Aphra Behn*, London, 1927, p. 50.

leaving Laurette's room, putting 'so many shillings on the mantelpiece'. Madame, the keeper of the house,

..... herself seeing Jacob out had about her that leer, that lewdness, that quake of the surface (visible in the eyes chiefly), which threatens to spill the whole bag of ordure, with difficulty held together, over the pavement. In short, something was wrong.   (pp. 103-4)

Virginia Woolf appears to feel that something has gone wrong in turning the most noble passion that can exist between man and woman into a commercial commodity. It is indulged in by the carbuncular clerk and the typist in 'The Waste Land' to while away boredom, and by Florinda, Laurette, and Fanny in *Jacob's Room* to earn money and to ward off the inner emptiness and the gnawing loneliness of life in a big city. This type of indulgence yields no happiness. The typist in 'The Waste Land' is 'bored and tired'. She is indifferent. While the clerk 'gropes his way, finding the stairs unlit', she smoothes her hair and 'puts a record on the gramophone'. Similarly in *Jacob's Room* when in the old house 'grained with human dirt' Jacob and Florinda come out of the bedroom door after 'the obscene thing', Florinda follows 'lazily stretching; yawning a little, arranging her hair at the looking glass'—a picture of boredom and indifference. Such circumstances as these in which both sexes cannot take what Baudelaire calls carefree pleasure in their blitheness, present a frightful picture, and rightly engender a sense of sin. Even Jacob, who wrote an essay on the Ethics of Indecency (p. 77), doubted whether he liked indecency in the raw (p. 81). Florinda and 'her sort', having this sense of sin, try to purify themselves, like Lady Macbeth, by 'washing the hands nightly before going to bed' (p. 78).

Talking like Sopwith—'talking, talking, talking—as if everything could be talked' (p. 39)—and discussing and pursuing useless subjects like Miss Marchant and Mr. Fraser (pp. 104, 107), instead of meditating silently like Mrs. Ramsay in *To the Lighthouse* and Bernard in *The Waves*, or being content to ruminate—which quality, as Nietzsche says in his Preface to *The Genealogy of Morals*, modern man lacks—make society mentally and spiritually ill. Miss Perry, aged sixty-six, Mr. Benson with a weak heart, and Miss Rosseter nursing a cancer, represent the senile, diseased, and decaying society of 'the time kept city'—London.

Believing with the poets, that a town, as contrasted to the country, is 'the sink of vice',[1] Virginia Woolf, thus describing the different aspects of 'hoary' London, makes it a symbol of modern civilization which she feels has gone wrong.

In search of a better civilization, Jacob, like D. H. Lawrence who went away to Mexico, leaves London for Paris, Italy, and Greece. In Paris he found only 'an awfully pleasant life'. It was full of 'extraordinary excitement'. The Italian civilization with its 'Villas among olive trees ..... men-servants watering cactuses. Black victorias ..... pompous pillars with plaster shields stuck to them' appeared to him a very inferior civilization about which he wanted to write an essay in the style of Gibbon. Therefore, as Virginia Woolf says elsewhere, 'it is to the Greeks that we turn when we are sick of the vagueness, of the confusion ..... of our own age',[2] Jacob turned to Greece. There the yellow column of the Parthenon firmly planted on the Acropolis, the pillars, the pediment, the Temple of Victory, and the Erechtheum set on a tiny rock, with their extreme definiteness, suggest 'ideas of durability, of the emergence through the earth of some spiritual energy elsewhere dissipated in elegant trifles (p. 147). The Parthenon, in its silent composure representing the ancient Greek civilization as compared to the 'new love songs rasped out to the strum of guitar and gramophone'—suggesting modern civilization, appears likely 'to outlast the entire world' (p. 148). It becomes a symbol of beauty and immortality. There in Greece Jacob stretched on the top of the mountain 'enjoyed himself immensely'. Probably he had never been so happy in the whole of his life. 'I intend to come to Greece every year,' Jacob wrote to Bonamy. 'It is the only chance I can see of protecting oneself from civilization' (pp. 143, 145). His being happy in Greece, and his desire to go there every year are symbolic of his acceptance of Greek civilization after repudiating modern civilization as represented by London—the 'hoary, sinful old city' with its 'hollow, sallow, fruitless days' (pp. 66,75).

Virginia Woolf in *Jacob's Room* says,

Though the opinion is unpopular it seems likely enough that bare

---

[1] *The Common Reader*, First Series, p. 25.   [2] Ibid., p. 59.

places, fields too thick with stones to be ploughed, tossing sea-meadows half-way between England and America, suit us better than cities

because not only are the cities sinks of vice, but also the society there teases and twists the 'something absolute in us'. She goes on:

There is something absolute in us which despises qualification. It is this which is teased and twisted in society. People come together in a room. 'So delighted,' says somebody, 'to meet you', and that is a lie. And then: 'I enjoy the spring more than the autumn now. One does, I think, as one gets older.' For women are always, always, always talking about what one feels, and if they say 'as one gets older', they mean you to reply with something quite off the point.

(pp. 143–4)

Therefore it is always away from cities that one finds peace and delight. It is in Greece with 'Hymettus, Pentelicus, Lycabettus on one side, and the sea on the other, as one stands in the Parthenon at sunset', when the sky is 'pink feathered, the plain all colours, the marble tawny in one's eyes', that one can feel 'the emergence through the earth of some spiritual energy'. It is again away from cities in Cornwall that one becomes conscious of 'peace and piety', and experiences a kind of ecstasy.

The mainland ..... wore an extraordinary look of calm, of sunny peace, as if wisdom and piety had descended upon the dwellers there. Now a cry sounded, as of a man calling pilchards in a main street. It wore an extraordinary look of piety and peace, as if old men smoked by the door, and girls stood, hands on hips, at the well, and horses stood; as if the end of the world had come, and cabbage fields and stone walls, and coast-guard stations, and, above all, the white sand bays with the waves breaking unseen by any one, rose to heaven in a kind of ecstasy.

(p. 47)

It is there in Cornwall and Greece that one comes across what Bernard Shaw, as reported by Virginia Woolf, called real human beings and not 'smudged copies' of them.[1] Virginia Woolf herself expressing somewhat similar idea says,

In six pages of Proust we can find more complicated and varied emotions than in the whole of the *Electra*. But in the *Electra* or in the

[1] *Diary*, p. 198.

Antigone we are impressed by something different, by something perhaps more impressive—by heroism itself, by fidelity itself. In spite of the labour and the difficulty it is this that draws us back and back to the Greeks; the stable, the permanent, the original human being is to be found there.

(*The Common Reader*, First Series, p. 44)

The shepherd of Greece in kilt, cap, and gaiters very nearly driving his herd of goats between the royal wheels, and the Greek women knitting in the shadow of the columns of the Parthenon, quarrelling, scolding, suckling their babes as jolly as sand-martins in the heat, like the Cornish girls standing, hands on hips, at the well, become symbols of uninhibited and natural human beings (pp. 147, 175). Their life is not squeezed and emasculated in a 'white satin shoe' like Clara Durrant's, or in the 'tight boots' of Madame Lucien Gravé (pp. 151, 150). They know no repression. On the contrary their life is free and expansive like feet in a 'pair of old shoes' (p. 176).

These natural and unconstrained people are carefree and relaxed. They are not lonely. Because their life, unlike that of the modern civilized man, has what Virginia Woolf calls all the elements of a perfect existence. Imagining some village, in a remote part of the country, near the sea, as a provisional background for Sophocles, she says,

Even nowadays such villages are to be found in the wilder parts of England, and as we enter them we can scarcely help feeling that here, in this cluster of cottages, cut off from rail or city, are all the elements of a perfect existence. Here is the Rectory; here the Manor house, the farm and the cottages; the church for worship, the club for meeting, the cricket field for play. Here life is simply sorted out into its main elements. Each man and woman has his work; each works for the health or happiness of others. And here, in this little community, characters become part of the common stock; the eccentricities of the clergyman are known; the great ladies' defects of temper; the blacksmith's feud with the milkman; and the loves and matings of boys and girls. Here life has cut the same grooves for centuries; customs have arisen; legends have attached themselves to hill-tops and solitary trees, and the village has its history, its festivals, and its rivalries. (*The Common Reader*, First Series, p. 40)

They have tradition. They have fellow feeling. Each works

for the health and happiness of others. Everyone is a part of the community, of the common stock. They are not lonely, because they are unlike the city multitudes who 'have no houses'. Describing the multitudes of London, she says,

The streets belong to them; the shops; the churches; theirs the innumerable desks; the stretched office lights; the vans are theirs, and the railway slung high above the street ..... A homeless people, circling beneath the sky whose blue or white is held off by a ceiling cloth of steel filings and horse dung shredded to dust.   (p. 65)

When the clock strikes six, these innumerable people jerking rapidly along the pavements, drop into darkness and are conveyed this way and that.

'Marble Arch—Shepherd's Bush'—to the majority the Arch and the Bush are eternally white letters upon a blue ground. Only at one point—it may be Acton, Holloway, Kensal Rise, Caledonian Road —does the name mean shops where you buy things, and houses, in one of which ..... there is a square curtained window, and a bedroom.   (pp. 65-6)

The shifting population of London spend their days in offices, and live their nights in curtained rooms. Unlike the villagers who, living in clustered cottages, lead a communal life, the multitudes of a metropolis living in bedrooms lead separate solitary lives. They do not belong to anyone or to anywhere. Having lost all relationship, they have ceased to be human.

At Mudie's corner in Oxford Street all the red and blue beads had run together on the string. The motor omnibuses were locked. Mr. Spalding going to the city looked at Mr. Charles Budgeon bound for Shepherd's Bush. The proximity of the omnibuses gave the outside passengers an opportunity to stare into each other's faces. Yet few took advantage of it. Each had his own business to think of. Each had his past shut in him like the leaves of a book known to him by heart; and his friends could only read the title, James Spalding, or Charles Budgeon, and passengers going the opposite way could read nothing at all—save 'a man with a red moustache,' 'a young man in grey smoking a pipe'.   (p. 63)

These unknown and unrelated persons, reduced to the status of tin soldiers and painted puppets with 'a man with a red moustache' and 'a young man in grey smoking a pipe' as their labels, become symbolic of lonely men.

Having shown the fruitless agitation of the lonely civilized man's life, Virginia Woolf shows its transitoriness by placing her characters against 'the broad-backed moors' and the Parthenon, which symbolize time and eternity. Human lives and their passions are short lived as compared to the moor and the Parthenon.

The columns and the Temple remain; the emotion of the living breaks fresh on them year after year; and of that what remains?

(p. 160)

The same sense of transitoriness Virginia Woolf declares through Julia Eliot who, while going to Lady Congreve,

had the rapt look of one brushing through crowds on a summer's afternoon, when the trees are rustling, the wheels churning yellow, and the tumult of the present seems like an elegy for past youth and past summers, and there rose in her mind a curious sadness, as if time and eternity showed through skirts and waistcoats, and she saw people passing tragically to destruction. Yet, Heaven knows, Julia was no fool. (p. 168)

This novel becomes melancholy because in it Virginia Woolf, thinking that 'it would be foolish to vex the moor with questions—what? and why?' (p. 133), does not either ask a question or try to explain life and death, as she does in *The Voyage Out* and the later novels. With the wanton death of Jacob, who is killed in the war, it becomes agitatingly depressing.

It becomes all the more distressing when we think that Jacob was the only one who not only repudiated modern civilization, but also wanted to solve the problem of civilization by writing an essay upon it. He was an intelligent distinguished looking young man who, as Bonamy thought, had something in him (p. 139). He was the only one out of the multitudes who would go home and read the *Byzantine Empire* by his fireside (p. 65). In his room were the classics and the Elizabethans. There were no Wells or Shaw or the sixpenny weeklies. If to have a room means, as Virginia Woolf herself says, to have the power to think for oneself,[1] then to have a room full of classics means to think about the lasting and the real. The death of a profound thinker such as Jacob, who might have helped to solve

[1] *A Room of One's Own*, p. 160.

the problem of civilization, therefore, is indeed very disturbing.

The only ray of hope in this darkness which drops like a knife, with the dull sounds 'as if nocturnal women were beating great carpets', symbolic of foreboding destruction, is the coming generation—Florinda is pregnant, there is a baby in the per-ambulator at Milton Dover House, Fanny Elmer has a little boy.

Jacob's Room is the first novel in which besides initiating the use of condensed symbols—such as Jacob's choosing the works of Byron in one volume, and London—Virginia Woolf has, like the Post-Impressionist painters, used colour symbolically. The pale yellow light, and something yellow-tinted and sulphurous like the dark and lemon yellow colours of Van Gogh's 'The Night Café', suggesting a 'devil's furnace of pale sulphur', and the purple sea, suggesting Phlegethon, the river of fire in Hades, become symbols of dread and fear. Similarly she employs astonishing agitation and vitality of colour to symbolize in-security and fear, and the white and purple colour of the bunches of grapes to symbolize innocence and passion.

This novel shows an appreciable improvement in her choice and use of symbols. Whereas in *The Voyage Out* and *Night and Day* the symbols employed—going out on journeys, the mist of London, the heat of South America, and rivers, trees and mountains—are mostly traditional and simple, in *Jacob's Room* they are mostly unconventional and more complex. The three geese, and the one bunch of white grapes and two of purple, are examples of the unconventional symbols used to evoke complex ideas.

CHAPTER FOUR

Mrs. Dalloway

VIRGINIA WOOLF started writing *Mrs. Dalloway* in June
1922, and completed it by October 1924, when the
after-effects of war—the maimed and the shell shocked,
the starving and the sick—were still affecting sensitive hearts.
These were 'the years of considerable human suffering', as
Leonard Woolf remarks in *After the Deluge*. The cause of this
human suffering, Virginia Woolf seems to feel, is the exploitation of man by man, be it political, economic, religious, or
social, whether 'in the heat and sands of India', in 'the mud and
swamp of Africa', or in 'the purlieus of London'. This exploitation is the outcome of the despicableness of society, which
Virginia Woolf tries to portray in this novel. Writing about it
in her diary, she says, 'I want to give life and death, sanity and
insanity; I want to criticise the social system and to show it at
work, at its most intense.'[1] Through *Mrs. Dalloway*, therefore,
Virginia Woolf delivers her diatribe against a superficial
society that lacks depth in human relationships.

To portray the different aspects of society Virginia Woolf
uses certain characters symbolically. Hugh Whitbread represents, as Sally Seton thinks, that which is 'most detestable in
English middle-class life'. He is a man who has 'read nothing,
thought nothing' (p. 81). He has the 'manners and breeding of
an English gentleman' (p. 9). He is a perfect specimen of 'the
public-school man', a great 'snob', who has married 'the
Honourable Evelyn' and found a little job at court.

He looked always as if he were on duty, thought Peter, a privileged
but secretive being, hoarding secrets which he would die to defend,
though it was only some little piece of tittle-tattle dropped by a court
footman which would be in all the papers to-morrow ..... Look at
him now, on tiptoe, dancing forward, bowing and scraping, as the
Prime Minister and Lady Bruton emerged, intimating for all the

---

[1] *Diary*, p. 57.

world to see that he was privileged to say something, something private, to Lady Bruton as she passed. She stopped. She wagged her fine old head. She was thanking him presumably for some piece of servility. She had her toadies, minor officials in Government offices who ran about putting through little jobs on her behalf, in return for which she gave them luncheon.   (pp. 189–91)

This 'admirable Hugh' who loves 'dressing up in gold lace and doing homage', and 'snuffing round the precincts of the great', besides representing a worldly careerist,[1] becomes symbolic of mental servility to plumed authority, and of unnatural loyalties, qualities which Virginia Woolf elaborates in *Three Guineas*.

The effect that all feel when 'greatness' passes by them also signifies the addiction of society to unnatural loyalties.

..... rumours were at once in circulation from the middle of Bond Street to Oxford Street on one side, to Atkinson's scent shop on the other ..... falling indeed with something of a cloud's sudden sobriety and stillness upon faces which a second before had been utterly disorderly. But now mystery had brushed them with her wings ..... But nobody knew whose face had been seen. Was it the Prince of Wales's, the Queen's, the Prime Minister's?   (p. 17)

The same 'dark breath of veneration' whether for Queen, Prince, or Prime Minister—the enduring symbol of the state (p. 19)—that ripples through glove shops and hat shops on both sides of Bond Street, ripples through everyone, and is felt 'to the marrow of their bones' when the Prime Minister—'this symbol of what they all stood for, English Society'—passes by them at Clarissa's party (p. 189). This worship of greatness for which the people are prepared to go 'to the cannon's mouth, as their ancestors had done before them' (p. 21), and are ready to open a bazaar, like Lady Bexborough 'with the telegram in her hand, John, her favourite, killed' (p. 7), becomes symbolic of the distortion of values which leads to unnatural loyalties, one of the causes of war and its inhuman destruction.

Miss Kilman represents possessive love and corrupt religiosity.

---

[1] Lord David Cecil in *Poets and Story-Tellers*, London 1949, p. 170, also remarks that Hugh Whitbread and Sir William are types of snobbish worldling and hard, power-loving careerist.

Bitter and burning, Miss Kilman had turned into a church two years three months ago. She had heard the Rev. Edward Whittaker preach; the boys sing; had seen the solemn lights descend, and whether it was the music, or the voices ..... the hot and turbulent feelings which boiled and surged in her had been assuaged as she sat there, and she had wept copiously ..... So now, whenever the hot and painful feelings boiled in her, this hatred of Mrs. Dalloway, this grudge against the world, she thought of God. She thought of Mr. Whittaker. Rage was succeeded by calm. A sweet savour filled her veins, her lips parted, and, standing formidable upon the landing in her mackintosh, she looked with steady and sinister serenity at Mrs. Dalloway, who came out with her daughter.   (p. 137)

Miss Kilman is religious not because she has had some vision or is poor in spirit and pure in heart, but because religion, like alcohol, serves as a means of escape from her gnawing anger and hatred. Her going to church, therefore, does not make her humble and tender. It makes her rather formidable and sinisterly serene. She wants to have mastery over others, to subdue them.

And there rose in her an overmastering desire to overcome her; to unmask her. If she could have felled her it would have eased her. But it was not the body; it was the soul and its mockery that she wished to subdue; make feel her mastery. If only she could make her weep; could ruin her; humiliate her; bring her to her knees crying, You are right!   (p. 138)

In her misplaced religious fervour Miss Kilman not only wants to humiliate and ruin Mrs. Dalloway, but also wants to possess and dominate Elizabeth. When Elizabeth prepares to leave after having finished her tea, Miss Kilman tries to prevent her. Prolonging her tea as much as possible, she says, 'I've not quite finished yet.' And when she had finally 'swallowed down the last inches of the chocolate éclair', her

agony was so terrific. If she could grasp her, if she could clasp her, if she could make her hers absolutely and for ever and then die; that was all she wanted.   (p. 145)

Virginia Woolf, like Rabindranath Tagore,[1] appears to have felt the sting of the domination of possessive love. That she loathed

---

[1] In *Gitanjali*, in Poem Number Thirty-Two, Tagore says: 'By all means they try to hold me secure who love me in this world. But it is otherwise with thy love which is greater than theirs, and thou keepest me free.'

domination of any type, especially of religiosity, is shown by her entry in her diary:

I meant to write about the Barnetts and the peculiar repulsiveness of those who dabble their fingers self approvingly in the stuff of others' souls ..... I come to loathe any dominion of one over another; any leadership, any imposition of the will.   (*Diary*, pp. 9–10)

These remarks provoked by her reading of *Rev. Canon S. A. Barnett: His Life, Work and Friends*, reflecting the integrity of her free unexploiting mind, throw light on her diatribe in *Mrs. Dalloway* against possessive love and dominating religion:

Love and religion! thought Clarissa, going back into the drawing-room, tingling all over. How detestable, how detestable they are! For now that the body of Miss Kilman was not before her, it over-whelmed her—the idea. The cruellest things in the world, she thought, seeing them clumsy, hot, domineering, hypocritical, eaves-dropping, jealous, infinitely cruel and unscrupulous dressed in a mackintosh coat, on the landing; love and religion.   (p. 139)

Miss Kilman, whose love is not unselfish, and whose religion is not pure, becomes a symbol of such impure sentiments as 'domineering', 'infinitely cruel', and 'unscrupulous' love and religion. As these are ugly and unpleasant things, Miss Kilman, who symbolizes them, is 'Ugly, clumsy' (p. 141), and shabbily dressed 'in a green mackintosh coat' (p. 14). Her mackintosh, therefore, as W. Y. Tindall rightly points out, 'inimical to waters, symbolizes her condition'.[1] It portrays, perhaps, the closed condition of her mind that does not allow any rain of grace to reach her parched heart.

An individual, as modern psycho-analytical research has shown, resorts to obsessional handwashing if there is a sense of guilt in his unconscious mind. Two examples of this are Pontius Pilate from history, and Lady Macbeth from literature, though Pilate was making a consciously symbolic act, and Lady Mac-beth an unconscious one. Similarly societies, at times, lay undue stress on outer neatness because of inner untidiness, on outer sense of proportion because of inner disorderliness, on outward show of strength because of inner weakness. Dr. Holmes and Sir William Bradshaw are symbols of such compensatory neat-ness, proportion, and order. They stand for that aspect of

[1] *Forces in Modern British Literature*, N.Y., 1947, p. 305.

human nature which Septimus thought was going to catch him, and to escape which he committed suicide. He felt

that human beings have neither kindness, nor faith, nor charity beyond what serves to increase the pleasure of the moment. They hunt in packs. Their packs scour the desert and vanish screaming into the wilderness. They desert the fallen. They are plastered over with grimaces .....

Once you fall, Septimus repeated to himself, human nature is on you. Holmes and Bradshaw are on you. They scour the desert. They fly screaming into the wilderness. The rack and the thumb-screw are applied. Human nature is remorseless.   (pp. 99, 108)

Sir William, the impress of whose will was received by the 'Naked, defenceless, the exhausted, the friendless', who swooped, and devoured, and who shut people up to appease the goddesses 'Sense Proportion' and 'Conversion' (p. 113), and Dr. Holmes are more powerful and overbearing, hence more harmful, than Miss Kilman with her possessive love and domineering religion.

Proportion, divine proportion, Sir William's goddess, was acquired by Sir William walking hospitals, catching salmon, begetting one son in Harley Street by Lady Bradshaw ..... so that not only did his colleagues respect him, his subordinates fear him, but the friends and relations of his patients felt for him the keenest gratitude for insisting that these prophetic Christs and Christesses, who prophesied the end of the world, or the advent of God, should drink milk in bed, as Sir William ordered; Sir William with his thirty years' experience of these kinds of cases, and his infallible instinct, this is madness, this sense; his sense of proportion.

But Proportion has a sister, less smiling, more formidable, a Goddess even now engaged—in the heat and sands of India, the mud and swamp of Africa, the purlieus of London, wherever in short the climate or the devil tempts men to fall from the true belief which is her own—is even now engaged in dashing down shrines, smashing idols, and setting up in their place her own stern counten-ance. Conversion is her name and she feasts on the wills of the weakly, loving to impress, to impose, adoring her own features stamped on the face of the populace ..... offers help, but desires power ..... concealed as she mostly is, under some plausible disguise; some venerable name; love, duty, self-sacrifice.   (pp. 110–11)

Sir William, therefore, shutting people up in his homes till they are converted to his point of view, becomes symbolic of egotistical sense of proportion and its forceful imposition.

The low, powerful, grey car of Sir William Bradshaw— the grey-haired doctor—with its grey furs and silver grey rugs, and his grey room, are also symbolical. Their greyness, reflecting the lack of warmth and colour of feeling, becomes symbolic of his insensitivity to human suffering (pp. 104, 105, 112). It also evokes a sense of dread, as does the dove grey upholstery of 'The Proime Minister's kyar' seen in Bond Street (p. 17). Whereas Miss Kilman is thought to be detestable only by Clarissa, Sir William is felt to be odious by Rezia, Richard, Clarissa, and Peter. Rezia had cried that 'she did not like that man' (p. 113). The Dalloways 'didn't like his taste, didn't like his smell' (p. 201). And Peter, seeing the Bradshaws at Clarissa's party, said, 'That they're damnable humbugs' (p. 212).

Similarly Peter Walsh, Sally Seton, and Septimus Smith are used symbolically to suggest the adventurous, the unconventional, and the visionary in society. As they cannot fit into the conventional society of London, one goes away to India, another lives in the country, and the third commits suicide. Thus they seek to escape being Londoners who, according to E. M. Forster, are only countrymen 'on the road to sterility'.[1] Both Peter and Sally, who are always friendly to each other, are unconventional and adventurous. It is through them that Virginia Woolf conveys her criticism of society, its hypocrisy and insincerity. In contradistinction to Hugh Whitbread and Sir William, they are interested in reading. Peter was interested, as Clarissa recalls, 'in Wagner, Pope's poetry, people's characters eternally, and the defects of her soul' (p. 9). Sally used to read Morris, Plato, and Shelley. They, along with Septimus who used to read Shakespeare and Dante, represent that class of educated men and women who made Sir William feel uncomfortable. For there was in Sir William 'a grudge, deeply buried, against cultivated people who came into his room and intimated that doctors, whose profession is a constant strain upon all the highest faculties, are not educated men' (p. 108). Cultivated, and with critical faculties wide awake, Peter and Sally are able to see through people. Peter was able to see

---

[1] *The Longest Journey*, London, 1924, p. 274.

through Clarissa's worldliness and pronounce that she had the making of, what he called, a 'perfect hostess' (p. 10). He was also able to judge correctly the faults and failings of Richard Dalloway and Hugh Whitbread. Sally, too, tried to 'get hold of things by the right end' (p. 81). She saw through 'the admirable Hugh—when Clarissa and the rest were at his feet' (p. 81) These two with their critical minds symbolize that minority of intelligentsia who are aware of the shortcomings of modern society.

Sally Seton had 'a sort of abandonment, as if she could say anything, do anything'; she could walk in 'quite unexpectedly without a penny in her pocket, one night after dinner'; she would run along the passage without a stitch of clothing, having forgotten her sponge, unmindful of gentlemen seeing her; she would smoke cigars, would paint, would write. Thus she becomes a symbol of freedom-loving rebels who break the rigid senseless conventionalities (pp. 37–38, 199).

Peter and Sally, being ordinary creatures with human failings, are ignored by society as of no consequence. But the brilliant and the visionary, because they do not follow the proportion of the herd, are pronounced mad. They are manacled, secured behind bars, or put in homes. If they still persist in their visions, they are crucified, poisoned, or forced to commit suicide. Septimus symbolizes those few who have been martyred because of their visions. Septimus was a promising young man who was 'anxious to improve himself'. His employer, Mr. Brewer, thought 'very highly of Smith's abilities' (p. 95). As the European war broke out, he was among the first to volunteer. He served with great distinction and was promoted. This bright young man is obsessed with his moral turpitude that he had not cared when his friend Evans was killed, and that 'he married his wife without loving her' (p. 101). He is also aware of the sins of society, the brutality blaring out on the placards, men trapped in mines, and women burnt alive, sights that would turn a sensitive mind mad.

Virginia Woolf, as she says in her diary, wanted *Mrs. Dalloway* to be 'a study of insanity and suicide; the world seen by the sane and the insane side by side—something like that'.[1] She has been successful to such an extent that the case of

[1] *Diary*, p. 52.

Septimus Smith can surely bear comparison with the cases of the insane described in scientific treatises on insanity. Septimus, like the insane mentioned by Bernard Hart in *The Psychology of Insanity*, exhibits undue excitement, then apathy, has hallucinations, and hears voices. Bernard Hart also points out that in many patients 'the reasoning powers seem to be in excellent order so long as they are applied to matters not immediately connected with the delusional system'.[1] Septimus Warren Smith in the same manner

could read, Dante for example, quite easily ('Septimus, do put down your book,' said Rezia, gently shutting the *Inferno*), he could add up his bill; his brain was perfect ..... (p. 98)

Yet whereas the modern psychologists are prone to think that the visions and trances manifested by 'the ascetics and ecstatics' being of 'frequent occurrence in the mentally disordered patients of today', are hallucinatory, Virginia Woolf, on the other hand, appears to share the classical viewpoint of Plato that '..... there is also a madness which is divine gift .....'[2] She feels that the so-called insane, who do not conform to the worldly proportion of the herd, sometimes have a better conception of reality, and have something useful to say. Septimus Smith, therefore, like Gérard de Nerval who, according to Arthur Symons, 'was only wise, passionate, collected, really master of himself, when he was insane',[3] and like Villiers de L'Isle-Adam who was 'an amusing kind of mad-man',[4] utters his profoundest sayings when he is thought to be insane. In a way Septimus seems to resemble Virginia Woolf herself. She had severe nervous breakdowns, and her mental stability was threatened for years by her brother's death. When Septimus had to utter his profound truths,

he muttered, gasping, trembling, painfully drawing out those profound truths which needed, so deep were they, so difficult, an immense effort to speak out. (p. 75)

Similarly Virginia Woolf used to feel very excited, especially when she was writing her novels of ideas. 'I get excited writing',

---

[1] Op. cit., Cambridge, 1957, p. 96.
[2] *Phaedrus, The Dialogues of Plato*, Vol. I, London, 1931, p. 449.
[3] *Confessions—A Study in Pathology*, N.Y., 1930, p. 2.
[4] Arthur Symons, *The Symbolist Movement in Literature*, London, 1908, p. 54.

she says at one place.[1] When she was writing what at that time she called *Two Guineas*, she reported,

I must very nearly verge on insanity I think, I get so deep in this book I don't know what I am doing. Find myself walking along the Strand talking aloud. (*Diary*, p. 268)

Similarly when she completed *The Waves*, she wrote,

I wrote the words O Death fifteen minutes ago, having reeled across the last ten pages with some moments of such intensity and intoxication that I seemed only to stumble after my own voice, or almost, after some sort of speaker (as when I was mad) I was almost afraid, remembering the voices that used to fly ahead. (*Diary*, p. 169)

So Septimus Smith, getting excited, talking aloud, seeing the dead, and hearing voices, utters such truths as Virginia Woolf pondered over throughout her life, and was to elaborate in her novels. 'There is a God ..... there is no death' (p. 28), '.... that trees are alive ..... and universal love' (p. 75), and time (p. 78) are some of the ideas in the mind of Septimus that Virginia Woolf later considered in *To the Lighthouse*, *The Waves*, *Orlando*, and *The Years*. Septimus Smith uttering these messages of universal love becomes a symbol of a visionary, and because he is not willing to conform to the sense of proportion, and refuses to be converted to the ideas of Holmes and Bradshaw, is a rebel against society. His flinging himself 'vigorously, violently down on to Mrs. Filmer's area railings' (p. 164), is not a sign of his being 'in funk' or a 'coward', as Dr. Holmes thought it to be. Like the 'self-Homicide' of the young man mentioned by De Quincey, it is a symbolic act of defiance, of refusal to be dominated and exploited.[2] He commits suicide to show that Bradshaw had no right to say 'must' to him, that Bradshaw had no power over him to

order rest in bed; rest in solitude; silence and rest; rest without friends, without books, without messages; six months' rest; until a man who went in weighing seven stone six comes out weighing twelve. (p. 110)

[1] *Diary*, p. 286.
[2] *De Quincey's Works*, Vol. VIII, Edinburgh, 1890, p. 403. In 'On Suicide' quoting Donne's *Biathanatos* in support of his argument that under certain circumstances 'self-Homicide' is not suicide, he mentions the case of a young man who looking upon imposition 'as an indignity to which he was determined in no case to submit', killed himself and died peacefully.

He did not want to be fattened like Dr. Holmes who, if he ever found himself even half a pound below eleven stone six, asked his wife for another plate of porridge at breakfast (p. 101), 'the large outline' of whose body Rezia saw against the window (p. 166). He did not want to have a large outline, symbolic of brute force, of well-fed bodies and starved souls. Believing, it seems, in the saying of Christ: 'What shall it profit a man if he shall gain the whole world, and lose his own soul', he thus, as Mrs. Dalloway feels, preserves his soul—'A thing ..... that mattered' (p. 202). Thus he is able to indict also, what Peter sarcastically calls, 'the triumphs of civilization' (p. 166). On another level this suicide of the shell shocked brilliant young man, Septimus, becomes an indictment of inhuman war.

Besides employing characters to give us an insight into the various aspects of society, Virginia Woolf uses them to symbolize certain conditions and states of mind as well.

And she watched out of the window the old lady opposite climbing upstairs. Let her climb upstairs if she wanted to; let her stop; then let her, as Clarissa had often seen her, gain her bedroom, part her curtains and disappear again into the background. Somehow one respected that—that old woman looking out of the window, quite unconscious that she was being watched. There was something solemn in it—but love and religion would destroy that, whatever it was, the privacy of the soul. The odious Kilman would destroy it.

(pp. 139–40)

The old woman free to do as she liked, to climb upstairs, stop, or gain her bedroom, and living alone by herself, safe from the domination of Kilman, becomes, for Clarissa Dalloway, who herself, in order to enjoy that privacy, had refused to marry Peter, a symbol of the privacy of the soul. She sees the old woman once again after she has heard about the suicide of Septimus:

in the room opposite the old lady stared straight at her! she was going to bed ..... It was fascinating to watch her, moving about, that old lady, crossing the room, coming to the window ..... It was fascinating, with people still laughing and shouting in the drawing-room, to watch that old woman, quite quietly, going to bed alone.

(p. 204)

The old lady quite quietly going to bed alone, unconcerned with the social gatherings, with the Holmes and Bradshaws making life intolerable, and the Smiths killing themselves, evokes in Clarissa once again the sense of the privacy of the soul that she wanted to preserve.

Just as in *The Voyage Out* Rachel's girlhood is symbolized by misty and cold London, the state of Clarissa's girlhood is externalized by the early morning air at Bourton, fresh, calm, and still, 'like the flap of a wave; the kiss of a wave; chill and sharp and yet (for a girl of eighteen as she then was) solemn .....' The time of the day and the surroundings, too, are symbolic. The early morning is suggestive of her youth—the morning of life—and the flowers and trees with the smoke winding off them, the rooks rising, falling, which she watches as she stands there with Peter, represent her feelings and aspirations about a rosy budding life. The rising and falling rooks become external symbols of the rising and falling emotions that she was feeling in the presence of Peter who loved her and for whom she had tender feelings (p. 5).

Like Clarissa, who thinks of the garden at Bourton when she thinks about her girlhood, Rezia, too, thinks about the Milan Gardens when she thinks of her maidenhood and happiness (p. 27). Once again she thinks of the garden and the country-side when she is given 'the sweet stuff' to drink to make her go to sleep. The quiet and peace, that descend on her as she drops off to sleep after those highly-strung moments of her life, are aptly externalized by the garden, the cornfields and the hills near the sea, and by the 'rain falling, whisperings, stirrings among dry corn, the caress of the sea', that she dreams about (p. 165).

Similarly the tender feelings of Richard Dalloway, and the freedom and delight of Elizabeth, are high-lighted by the mention of appropriate nature symbols. When Richard Dalloway, along with Hugh Whitbread, walks through the streets of London after having lunched with Millicent Bruton, he becomes conscious of the sham and strenuous life of London. 'For the worthlessness of life did strike Richard pretty forcibly .....' He desires rest and peace. He thinks about Norfolk, where

a soft warm wind blew back the petals; confused the waters; ruffled the flowering grasses. Haymakers, who had pitched beneath hedges to sleep away the morning toil, parted curtains of green blades; moved trembling globes of cow parsley to see the sky; the blue, the steadfast, the blazing summer sky.   (p. 125)

This restful landscape of Norfolk becomes symbolic of the feelings of rest and quiet which Richard Dalloway desired at that moment.

His daughter, Elizabeth, too, who had felt stuffy inside the Army and Navy Stores in the company of Miss Kilman, thinks about the country and dogs (p. 148). She wants to be out in the open air away from the oppressing presence of Miss Kilman. Therefore, when 'She was delighted to be free', the fresh air, symbolically, 'was so delicious' (p. 149).

The country, nature, and flowers, are used as appropriate symbols for the tender, peaceful, and quiet feelings of Peter, Sally, and Clarissa, also. Whenever Peter thought tenderly about Clarissa, and he thought about her quite often 'on board ship; in the Himalayas; suggested by the oddest things', he always was reminded of 'some field or English harvest', and he 'saw her most often in the country, not in London' (p. 169). And just as Sally 'despairing of human relationships' goes into her garden and gets 'from her flowers a peace which men and women never gave her' (p. 211), Clarissa gets her peace from the flowers in Miss Pym's shop.

There were flowers: delphiniums, sweet peas, bunches of lilac; and carnations, masses of carnations. There were roses; there were irises Ah yes—so she breathed in the earthy garden sweet smell as she stood ..... turning her head from side to side among the irises and roses and nodding tufts of lilac with her eyes half closed, snuffing in, after the street uproar, the delicious scent, the exquisite coolness. And then, opening her eyes, how fresh like frilled linen clean from a laundry laid in wicker trays, the roses looked; and dark and prim the red carnations, holding their heads up; and all the sweet peas spreading in their bowls, tinged violet, snow white, pale—as if it were the evening and girls in muslin frocks came out to pick sweet peas and roses after the superb summer's day, with its almost blue-black sky, its delphiniums, its carnations, its arum lilies was over; and it was the moment between six and seven when every flower—roses, carnations, irises, lilac—glows; white, violet red, deep orange; every flower seems to burn by itself, softly, purely in the misty beds; and how she loved the grey white moths spinning in and out, over the cherry pie, over the evening primroses!

And as she began to go with Miss Pym from jar to jar, choosing, nonsense, nonsense, she said to herself, more and more gently, as if this beauty, this scent, this colour, and Miss Pym liking her, trusting

her, were a wave which she felt flow over her and surmount that
hatred, that monster, surmount it all; and it lifted her up and up
when—oh! a pistol shot in the street outside!   (pp. 15-16)

Miss Pym's shop with its deliciously scented, exquisitely fresh
flowers burning by themselves, softly and purely, pleasurably
exciting the senses of smell, touch, and sight, with its neatness
and innocence heightened by the mention of the fresh 'frilled
linen from a laundry', and the 'girls in muslin frocks', and with
its visions of unruffled calmness evoked by the 'almost blue-
black sky', becomes symbolic of a haven where peace and
purity, seeping into 'the monster'—the leaf-encumbered forest
(p. 15)—Virginia Woolf's symbol for the soul—uplift a person
and help him to surmount the hatred and harshness of life
which are symbolized by the street outside with its harsh
metallic sounds of pistol shots. In contrast to London, which is a
symbolic setting for *Mrs. Dalloway* in which Virginia Woolf
wants to portray 'the despicableness of people',[1] and 'the
detestable social system', as Richard Dalloway calls it, the
flowers, gardens, countryside, and nature, mentioned in this
novel at different places, represent sanctuaries of peace.
Virginia Woolf seems to agree with Sally that one gets peace
not from men and women but from gardens and flowers, and
with North in *The Years*, that 'hills and trees accept one; human
beings reject one' (p. 435). Septimus Smith's message: 'do not
cut down trees', therefore, evoking these ideas, becomes
symbolic.

Some of the actions, too, in *Mrs. Dalloway* are of symbolical
nature. Peter Walsh's different actions with his old 'horn-
handled knife, which Clarissa could swear he had had these
thirty years' (p. 49), symbolize his various emotions and
attitudes of mind. His extraordinary habit of always playing
with his knife, that Clarissa had noted in him, stands for 'his
silly unconventionality, his weakness; his lack of the ghost of a
notion what any one else was feeling' (p. 52). His irritation on
thinking that having a Conservative husband was bad for
some women, is represented by his shutting 'the knife with a
snap' (p. 46). Similarly while he thinks about the life he had led
—full of 'journeys; rides; quarrels; adventures; bridge parties;
love affairs; work; work, work!'—as compared to the 'smugness'

---

[1] *Diary*, p. 55.

of Clarissa's life, he clenches his fist on his knife (p. 49). This clenching the fist on the knife like a Red Indian, evokes the most adventurous side of his life and personality. In the same manner his paring of his nails with his pocket-knife, and running his finger along its blade, suggest his mental attitude of being sharp enough yet to trim his life to his liking. He, as he told Clarissa, was going to his 'lawyers and solicitors, Messrs. Hooper and Grateley of Lincoln's Inn' to ask them to arrange a divorce for Daisy—'the wife of a Major in the Indian Army' —with whom he was in love (pp. 51–52). Again on leaving Clarissa, as he followed the 'young; quite young' woman wearing a red carnation, his straightening himself and 'stealthily fingering his pocket-knife' is symbolic of his need to reassure himself that he is still young and free (p. 59). Likewise his holding the knife at arm's length, viewing, and then replacing it in his pocket, are actions symbolic of his thoughts at that particular moment.

It was impossible that he should ever suffer again as Clarissa had made him suffer. For hours at a time ..... for hours and days he never thought of Daisy.

   Could it be that he was in love with her, then, remembering the misery, the torture, the extraordinary passion of those days? .....

   But then these astonishing accesses of emotion—bursting into tears this morning, what was all that about? ..... It was jealousy ..... which survives every other passion of mankind, Peter Walsh thought, holding his pocket-knife at arm's length. She had been meeting Major Orde, Daisy said in her last letter; said it on purpose he knew; said it to make him jealous; ..... he was furious! All this pother of coming to England and seeing lawyers wasn't to marry her, but to prevent her from marrying anybody else. That was what tortured him ..... when he saw Clarissa so calm, so cold . . . realising what she might have spared him, what she had reduced him to—a whimpering, snivelling old ass. But women, he thought, shutting his pocket-knife, don't know what passion is. They don't know the meaning of it to men. Clarissa was as cold as an icicle.

                                                                    (pp. 88–90)

This introspection about his own self, how he suffered when he loved Clarissa, how he feels about Daisy's love and about his own jealousy—this reviewing of his own personality—is aptly symbolized by the way he views his pocket-knife, holding it before him at arm's length. Thinking that women such as Clarissa, being as cold as an icicle, can neither know the sharpness of passion, nor understand it, he feels that he should not have made a 'snivelling old ass' of himself by showing his emotion to her. This feeling he externalizes by shutting the blade of his pocket-knife, and, it seems, replacing it in his pocket.

In the evening when he goes to attend Clarissa's party, on 'entering the house, the lighted house, where the door stood open, where the motor cars were standing, and bright women descending', Peter feels that 'the soul must brave itself to endure'. At that moment he opens 'the big blade of his pocket-knife' (p. 181). The opening of the big blade of his knife becomes symbolic of his braving himself to attend Clarissa's party, the type of party that he dislikes, and to face the humbugs he hates. This horn-handled knife, therefore, reflecting his thoughts, feelings, and attitudes, becomes a symbol not merely of his 'sex and intellect',[1] but of his personality as a whole.

Like the pocket-knife which symbolizes the personality of Peter Walsh, 'the green dress' becomes a symbol of Mrs. Dalloway's personality.

That was her self—pointed; dart-like; definite. That was her self when some effort, some call on her to be her self, drew the parts together ..... never showing a sign of all the other sides of her—faults, jealousies, vanities, suspicions, like this of Lady Bruton not asking her to lunch ..... Now, where was her dress?

Her evening dresses hung in the cupboard. Clarissa ..... gently detached the green dress and carried it to the window. She had torn it ..... By artificial light the green shone, but lost its colour in the sun. She would mend it ..... Where was the tear? .....

Quiet descended on her, calm, content, as her needle, drawing the silk smoothly to its gentle pause, collected the green folds together and attached them, very lightly, to the belt.   (pp. 42–44)

Her mending the dress, collecting the folds together, suggests her drawing her parts together and not showing the other side of her—faults, jealousies, vanities, suspicions—the tear in her personality. Therefore, as she brings the pleats of her personality together by forgetting the baseness of Lady Bruton in not asking her to lunch, by overcoming her hatred for Miss Kilman,

[1] W. Y. Tindall, *The Literary Symbol*, p. 116.

and by saying thank you, thank you to Lucy who was 'helping her to be like this, to be what she wanted, gentle, generous-hearted' (p. 44), quiet and calm descended on her. In this very effort of not showing a sign of the other side of her personality, and of appearing to be gentle and generous, there is something artificial, something tinselly. The green dress, therefore, that shines in artificial light but loses colour in the sun, becomes a suggestive symbol of 'the perfect hostess'.

Some of the ordinary things and happenings of everyday life, also, acquire added significance of a symbolic kind. The fountain where Peter and Clarissa meet

> was in the middle of a little shrubbery, far from the house, with shrubs and trees all round it. There she came, even before the time ..... the spout (it was broken) dribbling water incessantly .....
>
> She did not move. 'Tell me the truth, tell me the truth,' he kept on saying ..... She seemed contracted, petrified ..... She was like iron, like flint, rigid up the backbone. And when she said, 'It's no use. It's no use. This is the end' ..... it was as if she had hit him in the face.   (pp. 71–72)

The fountain with its broken spout and a dribble only, like the dry fountain in *The Voyage Out*, symbolizes the contracted and rigid feelings that Clarissa had at that moment for Peter.

Besides portraying the despicableness of society, and sanity and insanity, Virginia Woolf is interested in probing into the nature of life and death. Like Clarissa, she finds life

> In people's eyes, in the swing, tramp, and trudge; in the bellow and the uproar; the carriages, motor cars, omnibuses, vans, sandwich men shuffling and swinging; brass bands; barrel organs; in the triumph and the jingle and the strange high singing of some aeroplanes overhead .....   (p. 6)

Therefore

> a beating, a stirring of galloping ponies, tapping of cricket bats; Lords, Ascot, Ranelagh and all the rest of it ..... the bouncing ponies ..... the whirling young men, and laughing girls in their transparent muslins who, even now, after dancing all night, were taking their absurd woolly dogs for a run ..... discreet old dowagers ..... and the shopkeepers .....   (p. 7)

all giving her a sense of the divine vitality, become symbols of pulsating life. Similarly when Peter watches the beauty of

Bedford Place leading to Russell Square, he sees that

It was straightness and emptiness of course; the symmetry of a corridor; but it was also windows lit up, a piano, a gramophone sounding; a sense of pleasure-making hidden, but now and again emerging when, through the uncurtained window, the window left open, one saw parties sitting over tables, young people slowly circling, conversations between men and women, maids idly looking out (a strange comment theirs, when work was done), stockings drying on top ledges, a parrot, a few ordinary plants.

(pp. 179–80)

These ordinary things through their 'beauty pure and simple', giving him a sense of 'absorbing, mysterious', and infinitely rich life, attain symbolic value.

Clarissa Dalloway is concerned with the physical show of life that she sees in the swing, tramp, and trudge, in the bouncing ponies, in the whirling young men, and in the laughing girls in their transparent muslins. Not being interested, like Mrs. Ramsay in *To the Lighthouse*, and Eleanor Pargiter in *The Years*, in the 'inner' or the 'other' life, she remains, in spite of her occasional perfunctory musings about the soul and death, as Lytton Strachey felt, shallow and tinselly. Consequently her ideas about death do not attain the meaning and depth of Bernard's in *The Waves*. 'Fear no more the heat o' the sun', a line from *Cymbeline* which Clarissa often repeats,[1] symbolizes her conception of death. It is not something to be dreaded. If anything, it saves from the stresses of life. There is an 'embrace' in it, therefore one should not cling to life at the cost of one's integrity and personal dignity—'the thing that mattered', and which, as Clarissa thought, lay 'wreathed about with chatter, defaced, obscured in her life', and which she, like most social people, lets 'drop every day in corruption, lies, chatter'.[2]

[1] *Mrs. Dalloway*, pp. 34, 45, 154, 204.   [2] Ibid., p. 202

F

CHAPTER FIVE

To the Lighthouse

VIRGINIA WOOLF wrote *To the Lighthouse* 'to have father's character done complete in it; and mother's; ..... and childhood', as she mentions in her diary, and to have 'all the usual things ..... life, death, &c'.[1] Undoubtedly she has succeeded in recreating the atmosphere of her childhood, and in depicting the characters of her parents. Of Sir Leslie Stephen, Virginia Woolf writes:

His feats on the river and on the mountains had been won before they were born ..... He would start off after breakfast alone, or with one companion. Shortly before dinner he would return ..... and he scattered books round him in a circle. The thud of a book dropped on the floor could be heard in the room beneath. And often as he mounted the stairs to his study with his firm, regular tread he would burst, not into song, for he was entirely unmusical, but into a strange rhythmical chant ..... and the act of walking or climbing seemed to inspire him to recite whichever it was that came uppermost or suited his mood .....[2]

The relations between parents and children to-day have a freedom that would have been impossible with my father. He expected a certain standard of behaviour, even of ceremony in family life .....[3]

These, and many others, are the traits of Leslie Stephen's character which we find in Mr. Ramsay. Mrs. Ramsay portrays, in the same way, Julia, Virginia Woolf's mother, who 'took the keenest possible interest in young people ..... was happy in watching their friendships or love-makings'. Because of the help she used to render to the poor, she was remembered 'with affection and fervent gratitude' in the small, dingy, and crowded quarters of St. Ives. She was beautiful and was thought by some to look 'like the Madonna'.[4] There is a photograph taken by M. Loppé

---

[1] *Diary*, pp. 76–77.   [2] *The Captain's Death Bed*, pp. 67–68.
[3] Ibid., p. 71.
[4] F. W. Maitland, *The Life and Letters of Leslie Stephen*, London, 1906, pp. 323, 431, 324.

in which she is seen 'looking out of the window'. James Russell Lowell refers to her beauty in a poem addressed to Virginia Woolf in 1882:

> I wish her next, and 't is the soul
> Of all I've dropt into the bowl,
> Her mother's beauty—nay, but two
> So fair at once would never do.
> Then let her but the half possess,
> Troy was besieged ten years for less.[1]

According to Noel Annan, 'She responded to other people's feelings instinctively; she could heal a child's wound before it was given and read thoughts before they were uttered.'[2] Portraying all these facets of her character in Mrs. Ramsay, Virginia Woolf has created, as her sister Vanessa Bell thought, 'an amazing portrait' of their mother.[3] Yet, being a great writer, she could not be satisfied with merely creating a biographical novel concerned with the life and family of Sir Leslie Stephen. Like the great painters and artists who consider the great technicalities of painting and art as 'nothing but a noble and expressive language, invaluable as the vehicle of thought, but by itself nothing',[4] and who 'endeavour to express an idea rather than create a pleasing object',[5] Virginia Woolf has not only created pleasing portraits of Leslie and Julia Stephen in Mr. and Mrs. Ramsay, but also has used them as expressive symbols of some truth of her own conceiving. A close study of *To the Lighthouse*, therefore, like the contemplation of a great work of art, uncovers many layers of meaning. In this novel Virginia Woolf tries to suggest her ideas about reality and the intuitive understanding of it. She also endeavours to show how an enlightened person can help in overcoming silliness and strife which, she feels, are created by ugly academic jargon and dry intellection.

Virginia Woolf seems to think that intuition is something that women have and men lack and in the same way Mrs. Ramsay 'pitied men always as if they lacked something—women never, as if they had something' (p. 133). So Mrs.

---

[1] James Russell Lowell, *Last Poems*, London, 1895, p. 40.
[2] *Leslie Stephen*, London, 1951, p. 101.   [3] *Diary*, p. 107.
[4] John Ruskin, *Modern Painters*, London, 1903, p. 87.
[5] Roger Fry, *Vision and Design*, London, 1940, p. 243.

Ambrose in *The Voyage Out*, Mrs. Hilbery in *Night and Day*, and Mrs. Ramsay and Lily Briscoe in *To the Lighthouse* represent intuition, while Mr. Ambrose, Mr. Hilbery, and Mr. Ramsay stand for intellect.

Differentiating between two profoundly different ways of knowing a thing, Henri Bergson says:

The first implies that we move round the object; the second that we enter into it. The first depends on the point of view at which we are placed and on the symbols by which we express ourselves. The second neither depends on a point of view nor relies on any symbol. The first kind of knowledge may be said to stop at the *relative;* the second, in those cases where it is possible, to attain the *absolute.*[1]

S. Radhakrishnan, also, avers that intellect 'deals with relations and cannot grasp the relationless absolute'. He lays stress also on 'the inherent incapacity of intellect to grasp the whole.'[2] Virginia Woolf, too, thinking like these philosophers, says:

..... he could see, without wishing it, that old, that obvious distinction between the two classes of men; on the one hand the steady goers of superhuman strength who, plodding and persevering, repeat the whole alphabet in order, twenty-six letters in all, from start to finish; on the other the gifted, the inspired, who miraculously lump all the letters together in one flash—the way of the genius.   (*To the Lighthouse*, p. 58)

When describing Mr. Ramsay's mind, she writes:

It was a splendid mind. For if thought is like the keyboard of a piano, divided into so many notes, or like the alphabet is ranged in twenty-six letters all in order, then his splendid mind had no sort of difficulty in running over those letters one by one, firmly and accurately, until it had reached, say, the letter Q.   (p. 56)

This proceeding from A to B, from one letter to another, from one key on the keyboard to another, and not being able to lump all the alphabet together, besides standing for, 'the feeling of this frustration',[3] symbolizes the fact that intellect can comprehend relative points of view only, and that it is unable to grasp the whole. It fails to see reality, the absolute, the last

---

[1] *An Introduction to Metaphysics*, London, 1913, p. 1.
[2] *The Philosophy of the Upanishads*, London, 1924, pp. 51, 49.
[3] W. Y. Tindall: *Forces in Modern British Literature*, p. 304.

letter 'which is scarcely visible to mortal eyes, but glimmers red in the distance' (p. 57). Sir Leslie Stephen, too, was conscious of this fact: 'The Agnostic is one who asserts—what no one denies—that there are limits to the sphere of human intelligence.'[1]

The incapacity of intellect to see reality as a whole makes it blind to beauty: in a botanist it can count the tissues in a stem, or in a physicist it can explain the colour of a petal, but it cannot see the beauty of a flower as an artist can. Mr. Ramsay 'did not look at the flowers, which his wife was considering, but at a spot about a foot or so above them'. When he did notice them, he saw only 'something red, something brown' (p. 106). To Mrs. Ramsay he seemed

made differently from other people, born blind, deaf, and dumb, to the ordinary things, but to the extraordinary things, with an eye like an eagle's. His understanding often astonished her, But did he notice the flowers? No. Did he notice the view? No.

Therefore, when 'looking up, she saw above the thin trees the first pulse of the full-throbbing star, and wanted to make her husband look at it; for the sight gave her such keen pleasure', she stopped herself (pp. 111, 112). This trait in his character, along with the way he almost knocked over Lily's easel (p. 32), becomes symbolic of his aversion to beauty, as well as to the creation of it. Charles Tansley, too, lacks aesthetic sense. He would talk about his tie, rather than art and beauty, on his visits to picture-galleries (p. 18).

Unable to see beauty and realize truth, intellect remains interested in 'ugly academic jargon' (p. 24) and, unlike aesthetic creation, it lacks peace and reconciliation and produces restlessness. Mr. Ramsay's habit of walking up and down the terrace, alone or in the company of Charles Tansley, becomes symbolic of the restlessness of intellect.

The restless intellect has a way of 'peeling the flesh and blood off everything' (p. 18), and rending the thin veil of civilization. Devoid of human touch, like modern science and its discoveries, it becomes harmful and hurting, and shows 'astonishing lack of consideration for other people's feelings'. Both Mr. Ramsay and Charles Tansley are unmindful of the

---

[1] *An Agnostic's Apology*, London, 1893, p. 1.

feelings of others. When Mrs. Ramsay said that going to the
lighthouse depended on the weather being fine the next morning, James felt extraordinary happiness. But both Mr. Ramsay
and Charles Tansley dashed his spirits by asserting that it
would not be fine as the wind was due west (pp. 12, 14). Mr.
Ramsay, 'lean as a knife, narrow as the blade of one' (p. 12),
hurts his wife's feeling, too, by saying 'Damn you' to her
because she 'flew in the face of facts' by doubting his opinion
and saying that the wind often changed (pp. 53, 54). Sir Leslie
Stephen, according to Virginia Woolf, in order to express his
anguish, if ever a visitor threatened to stay not merely for tea
but also for dinner, used to 'burst out, half to himself, half to
the powers above, but quite audibly'.[1] Mr. Ramsay, like the
over-sensitive and nervously irritable Sir Leslie Stephen,[2]
talks aloud unmindful of causing embarrassment to the family,
and of hurting the feelings of the person present there. This trait
of Mr. Ramsay's character is pointed out at two places in this
novel. When poor old Augustus Carmichael asked for another
plate of soup, Mr. Ramsay 'was screwing his face up, he was
scowling and frowning, and flushing with anger'. Mrs. Ramsay
saw 'his anger fly like a pack of hounds into his eyes, his brow,
and she knew that in a moment something violent would ex-
plode' (p. 148). Again, while going to the lighthouse, when the
sails flapped and the boat made no motion at all, James and
Cam were afraid that Mr. Ramsay would lose patience in
a moment.

Sure enough, after fidgeting a second or two, he said something
sharp to Macalister's boy, who got out his oars and began to row.
But their father, they knew, would never be content until they were
flying along. He would keep looking for a breeze, fidgeting, saying
things under his breath, which Macalister and Macalister's boy
would overhear, and they would both be made horribly uncomfortable.   (p. 251)

Charles Tansley, too, who, according to Mrs. Ramsay, 'par-
odied her husband' (p. 29), hurts Lily's feelings by whispering
in her ear, 'Women can't paint, women can't write' (p. 78),

[1] *The Captain's Death Bed*, p. 69.
[2] F. W. Maitland, op. cit., p. 433, reports Sir Leslie Stephen as saying,
'I am, like my father, "skinless", oversensitive and nervously irritable.'

and by saying 'in a jerk, very rudely' to her that she would be sick if she went to the lighthouse (p. 135).

The other facet of this lack of feeling and understanding is selfishness and egotism which, being 'barren and bare', are always smiting like a 'beak of brass' or an 'arid scimitar' (pp. 62, 63). Lily Briscoe is aware of Mr. Ramsay's exactingness, and thinks that he never gives, he takes (pp. 231, 232). Thus dry intellection, discussing some branch of mathematics or philosophy, thinking about subject and object and nature of reality, and talking about Locke, Hume, and Berkeley, and lacking the milk of human kindness, brings ruin and chaos in its wake (p. 229). Mr. Ramsay's bringing ruin and chaos to Lily's painting, therefore, attains symbolic value and, possessing as he does a splendid mind, but lacking charity, tolerance, and kindness, he himself becomes an apt symbol of the intellect about which Virginia Woolf writes in her next novel:

..... the intellect, divine as it is, and all-worshipful, has a habit of lodging in the most seedy of carcases, and often, alas, acts the cannibal among the other faculties so that often, where the Mind is biggest, the Heart, the Senses, Magnanimity, Charity, Tolerance, Kindliness, and the rest of them scarcely have room to breathe.

(*Orlando*, p. 193)

Mrs. Ramsay and Lily Briscoe, on the other hand, symbolize the intuition—non-discursive immediate knowledge—that comes when one is completely forgetful of everything external as well as internal. Mrs. Ramsay

could be herself by herself. And that was what now she often felt the need of—to think; well not even to think. To be silent; to be alone. All the being and the doing, expansive, glittering, vocal, evaporated; and one shrunk, with a sense of solemnity, to being oneself, a wedge-shaped core of darkness, something invisible to others ..... and this self having shed its attachments was free for the strangest adventures. When life sank down for a moment, the range of experience seemed limitless ..... There was freedom, there was peace, there was, most welcome of all, a summoning together, a resting on a platform of stability.   (pp. 99–100)

All those who, sinking into themselves, have become free, can, like Mrs. Ramsay, know without seeing (p. 20) and comprehend without learning (p. 49). Similarly Lily Briscoe, who, having a few moments of nakedness like an unborn soul, bereft of body, unconscious of outer things—her name, her personality and her appearance (pp. 245–6)—can rise above herself, become capable of having visions (p. 86), and of seeing in a flash (p. 132).

In contrast with the analytical Mr. Ramsay who cannot see Z —symbol of reality—Mrs. Ramsay 'Sitting in Forgetfulness' like *Yen Hai*, is capable of that which Henry Bergson calls 'l'expérience intégrale'. In a state of 'samadhi'—transcendental consciousness—Mrs. Ramsay sees 'a coherence in things, a stability; something ..... immune from change', something that 'in the face of the flowing, the fleeting, the spectral' shines like a ruby (p. 163), and Lily Briscoe realizes that 'in the midst of chaos' there is shape, and that 'this eternal passing and flowing [is] struck into stability' (pp. 249–50). Lily, too, becomes conscious of 'life—startling, unexpected, unknown' (p. 277). This suggests that intuition alone is capable of what the Indian yogis call, 'anubhava'—integral experience—and the Zen Buddhists name 'Satori'—enlightenment—and thus confirms what Pascal says: 'the heart has its reasons of which the reason knows nothing'.[1]

Rufus M. Jones in his article on 'Mysticism' says that God, according to the metaphysics of Socrates, Plato, Aristotle, and Plotinus, is

Absolute Reality, Pure Being, Perfect Form, with no admixture of nature, i.e. with no potentiality or possibility of change. God is that which absolutely is, permanent, immutable, and free of everything that implies process of becoming.[2]

The oriental sages and seers, the writers of *Chhāndôgya-Upanishad* and the *Geeta*, also proclaim that God or Reality is 'Satya— that which is. He is Indestructible, immortal, unborn, Always-the-same.'[3] Virginia Woolf, like these Greek philosophers and Indian yogis, believes that behind all this Heracleitan fluidity and Bergsonian flux there is something stable and ever-lasting, something that the *Upanishads* call 'the still point of the turning wheel'. The hoary lighthouse, distant, austere, built on a rock, stark and straight, standing in a plateful of water (pp. 25, 286)—suggestive of fluidity and flux—becomes a

---

[1] *Pascal's Pensées*, London, 1931, No. 477.
[2] *Encyclopaedia of Religion and Ethics*, Vol. 9, Edinburgh, 1953, p. 84.
[3] Purohit Swāmi's translation of the *Geeta*, 1935, p. 22.

symbol of the Eternal and the Immutable. When Mrs. Ramsay
sees its light, then, like a mystic, she feels,

as if it were stroking with its silver fingers some sealed vessel in her
brain whose bursting would flood her with delight, she had known
happiness, exquisite happiness, intense happiness, and it silvered
the rough waves a little more brightly, as daylight faded, and the
blue went out of the sea and it rolled in waves of pure lemon which
curved and swelled and broke upon the beach and the ecstasy burst
in her eyes and waves of pure delight raced over the floor of her
mind and she felt, It is enough! It is enough!   (pp. 103–4)

This spiritual experience, or what T. S. Eliot would call 'the
intense moment', not only makes Mrs. Ramsay feel that
'Losing personality, one lost the fret, the hurry, the stir'
(p. 100), but also makes her realize her oneness with the
universe.

It was odd, she thought, how if one was alone, one leant to things,
inanimate things; trees, streams, flowers; felt they expressed one; felt
they became one; felt they knew one, in a sense were one; felt an
irrational tenderness thus ..... as for oneself.   (p. 101)

This suggests that ecstatic contemplation and intuitive comprehension of the changeless, releasing 'ecstasy' and 'pure
delight', can redeem one from miserable silliness and strife,
sterile egotism, vain ambition, and their attendant restlessness
to which Mr. Ramsay and Charles Tansley were easy preys.

'Shanti'—the peace of God, which is 'beyond our utmost
understanding'[1]—which is born out of the realization of the
absolute, imparts a halo, a glow. The dazzling beauty of the
Grecian, blue-eyed, straight-nosed Mrs. Ramsay, whose face
the Graces seemed to have composed 'in meadows of asphodel',
made the labourer leave his work and gaze at her (pp. 50, 28).
It sent Mr. Bankes into raptures (p. 77). Lily thought that 'her
face was all lit up—without looking young, she looked radiant'
(p. 157). To her husband she appeared 'astonishingly beautiful.
Her beauty seemed to him, if that were possible, to increase'
(p. 187). This symbolizes, what Radhakrishnan calls, 'Brahma-
tejas'—the radiance that the God-intoxicated have.[2] Lily, too,
had something of it. Her 'charm was her Chinese eyes' (p. 45).

---

[1] *New English Bible*, Philippians, 4, 7.
[2] *The Idealist View of Life*, London, 1951, p. 202.

The integrated personalities and the God-intoxicated people, like the 'Sanyasins' of India, do not lead an ivory tower life. Having realized their kinship with the universe, they dedicate their lives to the uplift of their community and the good of humanity. They swing, as Ruysbroeck says about the mystics, like a pendulum between contemplation and action, between adoration of God and service of man.[1] Mrs. Ramsay and Lily Briscoe, who have had their visions, live to serve others, to create unity and harmony, and to pacify and soothe the irritated nerves of modern intellectual society—the Ramsays and Tansleys of this world. Mrs. Ramsay insists that Minta should marry Paul and Lily Briscoe should marry William Bankes, and that Charles Tansley should also get married. This mania for marriages, as Lily calls it, symbolizes her instinctive desire to create unity, to turn 'I-I-I' into 'We'. By her mere presence at the dinner-table, Mrs. Ramsay merges them all into a party by bringing close all those who sat separate. No sooner does she leave the dining-room than the party breaks into separate groups again, and their talk turns from poetry to politics.

And directly she went a sort of disintegration set in; they wavered about, went different ways, Mr. Bankes took Charles Tansley by the arm and went off to finish on the terrace the discussion they had begun at dinner about politics, thus giving a turn to the whole poise of the evening, making the weight fall in a different direction, as if, Lily thought, seeing them go, and hearing a word or two about the policy of the Labour Party ..... (pp. 173-4)

After the death of Mrs. Ramsay, Lily once again feels that the house has become full of 'unrelated passions', and that there is chaos, because the unifying Mrs. Ramsay is not there (p. 230). Mrs. Ramsay has the power to bring this and that together, and to create something complete.

What they said she could not remember, but only she and Charles throwing stones and getting on very well all of a sudden and Mrs. Ramsay watching them ..... That woman sitting there, writing under the rock resolved everything into simplicity; made these angers, irritations fall off like old rags; she brought together this and that and then this, and so made out of that miserable silliness and

[1] Mentioned by Evelyn Underhill in *The Essentials of Mysticism*, London, 1920, p. 32.

spite (she and Charles squabbling, sparring, had been silly and spiteful) something—this scene on the beach for example, this moment of friendship and liking—which survived, after all these years, complete ..... and it stayed in the mind almost like a work of art.   (pp. 248–9)

Lily Briscoe, too, did not desire 'knowledge but unity' (p. 83). She, as an artist, produces balances between lights and shadows, creates relations of masses by connecting 'this mass on the right hand with that on the left', and does not want to break 'the unity of the whole' (p. 86). She avoids the awkward space in her painting by moving the tree to the middle (p. 132), and brings 'the wall, the hedge, and the tree' into harmony (p. 229). Similarly by eliminating the empty space by drawing a line in the middle, she is successful in creating harmony between the wall, the hedge, and the tree, and thus in making a perfect picture of her vision of life (p. 320).

Mrs. Ramsay and Lily Briscoe not only create unity and harmony but also, like the saintly people, radiate peace and have a calming influence. Mrs. Ramsay, 'the sponge sopped full of human emotions' (p. 54), 'delicious fecundity, this fountain and spray of life' (p. 62), in contrast to Mr. Ramsay and Charles Tansley, pacifies James by reading one of Grimm's fairy tales to him. When the shivering and quivering Mr. Ramsay wanted

to be assured of his genius, first of all, and then to be taken within the circle of life, warmed and soothed, to have his senses restored to him, his barrenness made fertile,   (p. 62)

Mrs. Ramsay was able to restore and renew him to the extent that he was able to go and 'watch the children playing cricket' (p. 64). In the same way Lily Briscoe pacifies the agitated Mr. Tansley by being nice to him, and thus helps him to 'expose and relieve the thigh bones, the ribs, of his vanity, of his urgent desire to assert himself' (pp. 142–3).

Besides conveying her ideas about intellect and intuition, Virginia Woolf wants to suggest her idea of 'the inadequacy of human relationship'. When Mrs. Ramsay became conscious of the fact that she had to hide many small things from her husband—that the mending of the green-house roof would cost fifty pounds, that his last book was not quite his best one—

she felt a very disagreeable sensation. She became aware of the
fact that her relationship with her husband could never give
her the pure joy of two harmonious notes sounding together
(p. 65), of being inextricably the same like waters poured into
one jar. Virginia Woolf emphasizes these feelings by making
Mrs. Ramsay remember the odious treatment that Mrs.
Carmichael had meted out to her husband in turning him out
of the house (p. 66–7). Mrs. Carmichael was unable to understand her husband, the poet, who, to Lily, looked like 'an old
pagan God, shaggy, with weeds in his hair, and the trident in
his hand' (p. 319). The Carmichaels and the fairy story of
the Fisherman and his Wife, which Mrs. Ramsay read to
James, become the symbols of the inadequacy of human
relationships of which Mrs. Ramsay had been conscious. The
inadequate relationship of the fisherman and his 'good Ilsabil',
who disagrees with him, symbolizes the flatness and dissonance
of human relationship (pp. 61–99).

Similarly, using other literary allusions symbolically, Virginia
Woolf suggests the moods and emotional reactions of her
characters. When Mr. Ramsay, pacing up and down the
terrace, grappling with some knotty metaphysical problems,
suddenly feels that his splendid mind, for all his efforts cannot
perform the arduous task of reaching Z—the last letter that is
scarcely visible to the mortal eye, but glimmers red in the
distance, he becomes aware of the limitations of his intellect
and conscious of his failure. Though it gives him 'the bleached
look of withered old age', yet, contrary to what W. Y. Tindall
says,[1] he does not feel dejected and frustrated. Even if 'All his
vanity, all his satisfaction in his own splendour' was shattered
and destroyed momentarily, he boldly 'rode and well, flashed
through the valley of death, volleyed and thundered—straight
into Lily Briscoe and William Bankes' (p. 52). He did not give
up his efforts, but tried 'to arrive at a perfectly clear understanding of the problem which engaged the energies of his
splendid mind' (p. 56). When he realized that he had 'stuck
at Q', feeling like the leader of a lost expedition, he decided
that 'he would not die lying down', but, 'his eyes fixed on the
storm, trying to the end to pierce the darkness, he would die
standing' (pp. 58–59). Therefore, his breaking out into 'some

[1] *Forces in Modern British Literature*, p. 303.

regular mechanical sound ..... something rhythmical half said, half chanted ..... something between a croak and a song', like Sir Leslie Stephen, and crying aloud 'Stormed at with shot and shell'—a line from 'The Charge of the Light Brigade'— acquires symbolical value. It expresses, as Bernard Blackstone points out, 'the feeling he has at the moment, of being the leader of a lost cause, worthy of pity but unflinchingly doing his duty',[1] thus giving us an insight into Mr. Ramsay's emotions and thoughts and evoking in us respect for him who, like the honoured Light Brigade, 'toiled honestly' (p. 59).

In the same manner Mr. Ramsay's saying 'Alone' and 'Perished' (p. 227) is not, as Bernard Blackstone imagines, a dramatization of his impatience at the delay caused by Cam and James in getting ready to go to the lighthouse. It symbolizes his emotions and the state of his mind at that particular moment of his life. Mrs. Ramsay is dead. He has been left 'a desolate man, widowed, bereft' (p. 256–7). He is getting decrepit and exhausted. He has failed to reach Z. At that moment his quoting from Cowper's 'Castaway' symbolizes that Mr. Ramsay feels that he is 'whelmed in deeper gulfs' beneath a rougher sea than was the castaway. It also suggests his determination to continue his intellectual pursuits. He reads a 'little shiny book with covers mottled like a plover's egg' (p. 282) even in the boat while going to the lighthouse. Like the castaway, who in the face of certain death did not abandon his manly efforts to swim through the engulfing waves, Mr. Ramsay does not give up his endeavour. Therefore, his murmuring, 'Some one has blundered' and 'We perished each alone', besides evoking the sense of chaos and loneliness, as described by Joan Bennett,[2] symbolizes unflinching resolution to pursue his intellectual quest.

At the conclusion of the dinner, when Mr. Ramsay starts singing 'Come out and climb the garden path' to Mrs. Ramsay, it sounded as if the words of the song were

floating like flowers on water out there, cut off from them all, as if no one had said them, but they had come into existence by themselves ..... the words seemed to be spoken by her own voice, outside herself, saying quite easily and naturally what had been in her mind the whole evening while she said different things. (p. 171)

[1] *Virginia Woolf, a Commentary*, London, 1949, p. 109.
[2] *Virginia Woolf—Her Art as a Novelist*, Cambridge, 1949, p. 104.

Everyone at the table was listening 'with the same sort of relief and pleasure that she had, as if this were, at last, the natural thing to say, this were their own voice speaking' (p. 172). This song thus becomes a symbol of their feelings. After the humdrum day, they were feeling restful in the soothing presence of Mrs. Ramsay. Lily Briscoe had had her vision of life which she would be able to express on her canvas by moving 'the tree to the middle' (pp. 132–5). She also had relieved Mr. Tansley of his egotism, vanity, and his urgent desire to assert himself. She had been kind and nice to him (p. 144). Minta had a glow; she had become engaged to Paul Rayley who, too, was 'glowing and burning' (pp. 153, 158). Minta's glow had infected Mr. Ramsay: 'not burdened, not weighed down with the greatness of his labours and the sorrows of the world and his fame or his failure .....' he looked 'astonishingly young' (p. 154). He was in 'great spirits' and wished 'to make it all right with old Augustus after that scene about the soup' (p. 170). Augustus Carmichael also was happy and singing, and having forgotten his indifference to Mrs. Ramsay, 'turned slightly towards her ..... and bowed to her as if he did her homage' (p. 172). And to crown it all William Bankes, whom she was able to detain for dinner, after attentively eating the rich and tender Boeuf en Daube, had said, 'It is a triumph.' And for the wonderful woman, Mrs. Ramsay, 'all his love, all his reverence had returned' (p. 156). Life was thus happy and peaceful. In the song which Carmichael sings, the triumphant Kings 'riding by over lawn and daisy lea' suggest glory and peace. The beauty and happiness of life is symbolized by the China rose that is 'all abloom and buzzing with the yellow bee' (pp. 171–2).

Another literary allusion used symbolically is the Shakespearean sonnet, 'From you have I been absent in the spring', which Mrs. Ramsay reads while sitting in her husband's study. As she entered the study she felt

she had to come there to get something she wanted. First she wanted to sit down in a particular chair under a particular lamp. But she wanted something more, though she did not know, could not think what it was that she wanted.   (p. 181)

And again she thought

There is something I want—something I have come to get, and she fell deeper and deeper without knowing what it was. (p. 183)

It was then that 'she turned and felt on the table beside her for a book', and started reading here and there at random. The sonnet which says that without the beloved 'proud-pied April' with all its different flowers in odour and hue seems 'winter' to the lover, expresses Mrs. Ramsay's love for her husband which she could not express verbally. Her husband reproached her and called her 'a heartless woman' because she 'never could say what she felt' (p. 190). 'But it was not so'—by making Mrs. Ramsay read that particular sonnet, Virginia Woolf reveals to the reader that '—it was not so' (p. 190). This is what Mrs. Ramsay wanted to tell her husband—that she loved him, and that she was not a heartless woman. She also wanted to reach the state of feeling 'Nothing on earth can equal this happiness', which she did reach in the end (p. 191).

Virginia Woolf also uses allusions from religion, and religious art, to evoke the reverence that the various characters in the novel feel. After having seen Mrs. Ramsay sitting with James in the window with a rapture equivalent to the loves of dozens of young men, William Bankes saw Lily's painting of Mrs. Ramsay reading to James, and he thought of Raphael's Mother and Child—objects of universal veneration. This allusion, therefore, becomes a symbol of Mr. Bankes's veneration for Mrs. Ramsay (pp. 85, 272). In the same way Mr. Ramsay's sharing bread and cheese with the old fisherman and his son becomes symbolic. It suggests Christ's breaking bread with the fishermen and evokes in us the respect that James and Cam felt for their father. Cam thought 'This is right, this is it', and she felt, 'as she did in the study when the old men were reading *The Times*' (p. 314), that 'he was most lovable, he was most wise, he was not vain or a tyrant' (p. 291). Thus, because Mr. Ramsay's eating bread and cheese with the old fisherman, has a religious significance, it summons up Cam's old feelings of love and admiration for her father, and helps her to break away from the vowed pact she had made with her brother against him.

Trees and birds, too, like character and allusion, attain symbolic value in *To the Lighthouse*. William Bankes, unlike Mr. Ramsay, was not one of those men 'who do their best work before they are forty' (p. 41). He was capable of his best even when he was old enough to be Lily's father (p. 33). Lily Briscoe admired him, and, as they came to pause by the pear tree, said silently, 'I respect you ..... in every atom; you are not vain; you are entirely impersonal; you are finer than Mr. Ramsay; you are the finest human being that I know ..... praise would be an insult to you, generous, pure-hearted, heroic man!' (p. 42). The long-lived pear tree that is known to have borne fruit even though 300 years old becomes a symbol of the utility and vigour which Lily Briscoe associated with William Bankes. The same pear tree reminds Lily Briscoe of Mr. Ramsay's splendid mind. Lodged in the fork of the pear tree she sees 'a phantom kitchen table, one of those scrubbed board tables, grained and knotted, whose virtue seems to have been laid bare by years of muscular integrity' (p. 41). The kitchen table, reminding one of Sir Leslie Stephen's 'This is a table',[1] becomes a symbol, as Andrew had pointed out to Lily, of Mr. Ramsay's intellection (p. 40).

In *Jacob's Room*, Virginia Woolf used the symbol of three geese (see p. 42 above). In *To the Lighthouse* she employs a hen straddling her wings to protect her chicks as a symbol.

Looking at the far sand hills, William Bankes thought of Ramsay: thought of a road in Westmorland, thought of Ramsay striding along a road by himself hung round with that solitude which seemed to be his natural air. But this was suddenly interrupted, William Bankes remembered (and this must refer to some actual incident), by a hen, straddling her wings out in protection of a covey of little chicks, upon which Ramsay, stopping, pointed his stick and said 'Pretty—pretty,' an odd illumination into his heart, Bankes had thought it, which showed his simplicity, his sympathy with humble things; but it seemed to him as if their friendship had ceased, there, on that stretch of road.   (p. 37)

Mr. Ramsay's saying 'Pretty—pretty' not only gave Mr. Bankes an odd illumination about Ramsay's being simple and sympathetic to humble beings, but also gave him an insight into his unconscious desire to have a wife and children. In Ramsay's desire for fluttering wings and clucking domesticities he saw the end of their friendship.

'Time Passes', the second section of *To the Lighthouse*, is, as

[1] 'What is Materialism?', *An Agnostic's Apology*, London, 1893, p. 137.

Virginia Woolf herself felt, a 'difficult abstract piece of writing ..... all eyeless and featureless with nothing to cling to'.[1] It primarily aims at suggesting the passage of time by describing an empty house. As the scene changes from the fullness and warmth of a throbbing house inhabited by Mrs. Ramsay, her family, and friends, to the cold emptiness of a neglected house, the quality of the symbol employed also changes with it. In this section, instead of character and allusion she employs atmosphere and nature as symbols.

So with the lamps all put out, the moon sunk, and a thin rain drumming on the roof a down-pouring of immense darkness began. Nothing, it seemed, could survive the flood, the profusion of darkness which, creeping in at keyholes and crevices, stole round window blinds, came into bedrooms, swallowed up here a jug and basin, there a bowl of red and yellow dahlias, there the sharp edges and firm bulk of chest of drawers .....
  Nothing stirred in the drawing-room or in the dining-room or on the staircase. Only through the rusty hinges and swollen sea-moistened wood-work certain airs, detached from the body of the wind (the house was ramshackle after all) crept round corners and ventured indoors ..... Then smoothly brushing the walls, they passed on musingly ..... they went to the window on the staircase, to the servants' bedrooms, to the boxes in the attics ..... At length, desisting, all ceased together, all sighed together; all together gave off an aimless gust of lamentation to which some door in the kitchen replied; swung wide; admitted nothing; and slammed to.

(pp. 195–7)

The immense darkness, that swallows up here a jug and basin, there a bowl of dahlias, and the prying airs that, like the yellow fog and smoke in 'The Love Song of J. Alfred Prufrock', slip into the empty house, and sigh and lament together, create an atmosphere that suggests the emptiness of the house, and its lack of warmth and life. Similarly 'the torment of storms', and the tumbling and tossing of the 'gigantic chaos', and the lunging and plunging of 'the winds and waves', and 'the arrow-like stillness' of the spring day, 'eyeless and thus terrible', also evoke a sense of weird emptiness (pp. 208–9).
  Virginia Woolf suggests the passage of time by describing both the condition of the interior of the house, and the state of

[1] *Diary*, p. 88.

affairs outside it. The wild growth of poppies among the dahlias, of giant artichokes among roses, of fringed carnations among cabbages, and of the long grass suggests years of neglect (p. 213). Inside, the rusty hinges, the swollen sea-moistened wood-work, the fading roses on the wall paper (p. 196), the mouldy books, the moth-eaten clothes, and the shovelfuls of fallen plaster, represent the passage of time (pp. 209–13). The uninhabited decaying house on the verge of plunging 'to the depths to lie upon the sands of oblivion', like Mrs. McNab and Mrs. Bast who creaked and groaned, becomes a symbol of the passage of time (p. 215).

Autumn, spring, and summer, the different seasons, besides symbolizing the passage of time, externalize the various moods and emotions of the different characters.

The autumn trees, ravaged as they are, take on the flash of tattered flags kindling in the gloom of cool cathedral caves where gold letters on marble pages describe death in battle and how bones bleach and burn far away in Indian sands .....

The nights now are full of wind and destruction; the trees plunge and bend and their leaves fly helter skelter until the lawn is plastered with them and they lie packed in gutters and choke rain pipes and scatter damp paths.   (pp. 198–9)

The ravaged autumn trees like tattered flags become a symbol of Mr. Ramsay who, because of his wife's death, is left widowed and bereft; and the leaves flying hither and thither, and the choked rain pipes, symbolize the confusion of his mind and his choked emotions. Similarly the spring 'bare and bright like a virgin fierce in her chastity, scornful in her purity' and 'entirely careless of what was done or thought by beholders', becomes a symbol of Prue Ramsay.[1] She 'was given in marriage that May', and, as people said, she looked beautiful. Her happiness, like spring, was short lived. She died that summer in some illness connected with childbirth (pp. 204–5). And the heat of summer with its 'ominous sounds like the measured blows of hammers dulled on felt', its silence broken by the shrieking aloud of 'a giant voice' and 'the thud of something falling', symbolizes the death of Andrew Ramsay in the prime of his youth (pp. 206–7).

[1] Virginia Woolf, it seems, modelled Prue after her step-sister Stella Duckworth who was married in April and died in July 1897.

CHAPTER SIX

Orlando

TALKING about *Orlando*, David Daiches says, 'It would be a weary task to disentangle the profoundly symbolic from the deliberately irresponsible .....',[1] and, I would add, the historically true. Yet it is a fascinating study to see how from the available factual material Virginia Woolf has created a delightful novel, though, like Defoe and Fielding who name their novels 'The Life, Adventures and Pyracies of .....', and 'The History of .....', she calls it 'A Biography'.

It is based upon Victoria Sackville-West, Knole, and the Sackvilles. The heraldic leopard, the swaying tapestry, the gilded furniture, and the depth of mirrors that Virginia Woolf mentions in *Orlando*, are directly taken from Victoria Sackville-West's book *Knole and the Sackvilles*.[2] Hall, the falconer; Giles, the groom; Mrs. Grimsditch, the house-keeper; and Mr. Dupper, the chaplain, are all in *Knole and the Sackvilles* having their dinner at the Parlour Table or the Long Table of 'the Right Honourable Richard, Earl of Dorset, in the year of our Lord 1613'.[3] The character and temperament of Orlando changes according to the temperaments of the various Sackvilles who lived during the different ages—the Elizabethan, the Restoration, and the Victorian—and he/she reflects their several tastes and pleasures. *Orlando* no doubt is, as Stephen Spender says, 'a fantastic meditation on a portrait of Victoria Sackville-West'.[4] In spite of all this it is not a merely biographical novel. Just as *To the Lighthouse* goes beyond the biographical notes of Sir Leslie Stephen and his family to reflect Virginia Woolf's ideas about 'reality' and its intuitive realization, *Orlando*, besides fantastically portraying the Sackville-West family,

---

[1] *The Novel and the Modern World*, The University of Chicago Press, 1939, p. 185.

[2] London, 1922.   [3] Op. cit., pp. 78, 80.

[4] *World Within World*, London, 1951, p. 152.

symbolizes Virginia Woolf's ideas about time, personality, literature, and the art of biography.

Orlando begins with the closing reign of Queen Elizabeth who was growing 'old and worn and bent' (p. 24), and closes on 'the twelfth stroke of midnight, Thursday, the eleventh of October, Nineteen hundred and Twenty Eight' (p. 295). Orlando, its protagonist, living through this long period—more than three hundred years—attains the age of thirty-six years. This extraordinary discrepancy symbolizes Virginia Woolf's idea about the two different ages of man, which are determined by 'time on the clock and time in the mind', and not by a sort of 'bogus "time"' which, according to Wyndham Lewis, the Bloomsbury people have created 'to take the place of the real "Time"'.[1] Writing about time, Virginia Woolf says:

..... time, unfortunately, though it makes animals and vegetables bloom and fade with amazing punctuality, has no such simple effect upon the mind of man. The mind of man, moreover, works with equal strangeness upon the body of time. An hour, once it lodges in the queer element of the human spirit, may be stretched to fifty or a hundred times its clock lengths; on the other hand, an hour may be accurately represented on the timepiece of the mind by one second.   (*Orlando*, p. 91)

So of Orlando she writes that it 'would be no exaggeration to say that he would go out after breakfast a man of thirty and come home to dinner a man of fifty-five at least' (p. 92).

The age of a person, as determined by 'time in the mind' varies according to the poetic temperament and the imaginative faculty of that person. The unimaginative, she feels, 'live precisely the sixty-eight or seventy-two years allotted them on the tombstone'. Imaginative people

are hundreds of years old though they call themselves thirty-six. The true length of a person's life, whatever the *Dictionary of National Biography* may say, is always a matter of dispute.

(*Orlando*, pp. 274–5)

Orlando who, being modelled after Victoria Sackville-West, is a poet and thirty-six years of age according to the time on the clock, is more than three hundred years old according to the time in the mind. Victoria Sackville-West had evidently

[1] *Men Without Art*, London, 1934, p. 167.

lived the past in her imagination because in addition to *Knole and the Sackvilles* she wrote, at the age of thirteen, 'an enormous novel' about Edward Sackville and his two sons. She loved Knole, and in the old house 'the past mingled with the present .....'[1]

The house is not haunted, but you require either an unimaginative nerve or else a complete certainty of the house's benevolence before you can wander through the state-rooms after nightfall with a candle. The light gleams on the dull gilding of furniture and into the misty depths of mirrors, and startles up a sudden face out of the gloom; something creaks and sighs; the tapestry sways, and the figures on it undulate and seem to come alive.[2]

This quality of having lived the past imaginatively Virginia Woolf portrays symbolically by making Orlando a fantastic character who lives through the Elizabethan, Restoration and Victorian ages and yet is only thirty-six in nineteen hundred and twenty-eight.

De Quincey compares the human brain to a palimpsest:

What else than a natural and mighty palimpsest is the human brain? Such a palimpsest ..... oh reader! is yours. Everlasting layers of ideas, images, feelings, have fallen upon your brain softly as light. Each succession has seemed to bury all that went before. And yet, in reality, not one has been extinguished.[3]

Virginia Woolf appears to agree with De Quincey that ideas, images, feelings, like the words on a palimpsest, continue to live in one's brain. While writing about William Hazlitt in 1930, only two years after the publication of *Orlando*, she says,

He loves to grope among the curious depths of human psychology and to track down the reason of things. He excels in hunting out the obscure causes that lie behind some common saying or sensation, and the drawers of his mind are well stocked with illustrations and arguments ..... He is speaking of what he knows from experience when he exclaims, 'How many ideas and trains of sentiments, long and deep and intense, often pass through the mind in only one day's thinking or reading!' Convictions are his life blood; ideas have formed in him like stalactites, drop by drop, year by year.[4]

[1] *Knole and the Sackvilles*, pp. 82–83.   [2] Ibid., pp. 14–15.
[3] *De Quincey's Works*, Vol. XIII, Edinburgh, 1890, p. 346.
[4] 'William Hazlitt', *The Times Literary Supplement*, 18 September 1930, p. 722.

Orlando's fantastic age represents the idea that the impressions gathered by Victoria Sackville-West and the emotions she experienced while walking through Knole at night with a taper in her hand and while musing in the family chapel alone, formed into imperishable stalactites and left an indelible imprint on the palimpsest of her mind.

Orlando's being as old as the Sackville family suggests another train of thought. In *Mrs. Dalloway* and *To the Lighthouse*, two novels immediately preceding *Orlando*, and in *The Waves*, immediately following it, Virginia Woolf repeats her idea about the continuance of life after death. Clarissa Dalloway feels that she will survive in the trees at home and in the house there, in other people, and especially in the people she knew best.[1] Mrs. Ramsay believes that she will survive in others as long as they live.[2] Bernard puts it more pithily when he says, 'we are the continuers, we are the inheritors'.[3] By making the long line of the Earls and Dukes of Dorset and the Lord Sackvilles live in Orlando Virginia Woolf makes him a symbol, if not of the whole racial and collective unconscious described by Jung, at least of that part of it which we may name 'the family unconscious'. All these ideas make the fantasy about Orlando's age highly symbolical.

Orlando's change of sex, also, is used symbolically to suggest another group of ideas. In *Symbols of Transformation* Jung mentions that 'Amon the primordial water which was in the beginning' was known as 'the father of fathers, the mother of mothers'. He also mentions that in Egyptian and Babylonian mythologies the 'generative primal matter' and 'the primordial mother' are both bisexual by nature. Talking about 'anima' Jung says,

Since the anima is an archetype that is found in men, it is reasonable to suppose that an equivalent archetype must be present in women; for just as the man is compensated by a feminine element, so woman is compensated by a masculine one.[4]

In support of his thesis he quotes Edward Maitland and Nicholas of Flüe, two Christian mystics, who saw reality in a

---

[1] *Mrs. Dalloway*, pp. 11–12.   [2] *To the Lighthouse*, p. 17.
[3] *The Waves*, p. 183.
[4] *AION: Researches into the Phenomenology of the Self, The Collected Works of C. G. Jung*, Vol. 9, Part II, London, 1959, p. 14.

bisexual form—'Mother as well as Father', and as 'majestic father', and 'majestic mother'. Poets and philosophers, too, have believed in the androgynous state of man. Virginia Woolf herself, while discussing the 'Unity of mind', questions 'whether there are two sexes in the mind corresponding to the two sexes in the body'. She comes to the conclusion that

in each one of us two powers preside, one male, one female; and in the man's brain the man predominates over the woman, and in the woman's brain the woman predominates over the man.

(*A Room of One's Own*, p. 147)

This idea of a person's being both 'Hee and Shee', Virginia Woolf also mentions in *The Waves*, though on a slightly different plane, when she makes Bernard say, 'nor do I always know if I am man or woman' (p. 199). Orlando's being first a man and then a woman, besides suggesting man's being androgynous, represents the change in the historical character represented by Orlando.

It was a change in Orlando herself that dictated her choice of a woman's dress and of a woman's sex ..... Different though the sexes are, they intermix. In every human being a vacillation from one sex to the other takes place ......

For it was this mixture in her of man and woman ..... that often gave her conduct an unexpected turn. The curious of her own sex would argue, for example, if Orlando was a woman, how did she never take more than ten minutes to dress? And were not her clothes chosen rather at random, and sometimes worn rather shabby? ..... Yet again, they noted, she detested household matters, was up at dawn and out among the fields in summer before the sun had risen. No farmer knew more about the crops than she did. She could drink with the best and liked games of hazard.   (pp. 171-2)

This lack of a feminine concern for clothes, and having a manly interest in farming, drinks and games of hazard, show the predominance of man in Orlando. But at another time the feminine in her—giving birth to and bringing up children, and the running of the household, as represented by her buying 'sheets for a double bed' (p. 271) becomes uppermost.

In *Knole and the Sackvilles* Victoria Sackville-West, describing Charles, the Sixth Earl, says,

..... let us call him the Restoration Earl—the jolly, loose-living, magnificent Maecenas, 'during the whole of his life the patron of men of genius and the dupe of women, and bountiful beyond measure to both' ..... he disturbed London by a rowdy youth; he was reported to have passed on his mistresses to the king .....

(p. 115)

When it comes to John Frederick Sackville, she describes him as follows:

He belonged to an age more delicate, more exquisite; an age of quizzing glasses, of flowered waistcoats, of buckled shoes, and of slim bejewelled swords.   (pp. 176–7)

A little earlier in that book she also mentions how the rowdy way of life of the Restoration had changed to the 'good breeding, decency of manners, and dignity of exterior deportment of Queen Anne's time' (p. 152). This change in the Sackvilles from the robust masculine to the delicate more feminine behaviour of a later age along with the fact that on the death of the Duchess Arabella Diana 'her estate devolved upon her two daughters, Mary and Elizabeth'—from male to female descendants— are other points of significance in Orlando's change of sex.

In *Orlando* the house, nine acres of stone (p. 70), massed like a town with 'stables, kennels, breweries, carpenters' shops, wash-houses, places where they make tallow candles, kill oxen, forge horse-shoes, stitch jerkins' (p. 19), like the broad-backed moors and the Parthenon in *Jacob's Room*, and like the house and the 'Noble Barn' in *Between the Acts*, becomes a symbol of historical time against which Virginia Woolf shows the passage of different ages. The house and the oak tree still stand after generations of Sackvilles, having played their parts, have departed. Virginia Woolf seems to believe with Sir Thomas Browne, whom she mentions in *Orlando*, that 'the irregularities of vain-glory, and wilde enormities of ancient magnanimity ..... must diminish their diameters and be poorly seen in Angles of Contingency'.[1] She externalizes this idea by describing the crypt of the family chapel, where Orlando's ancestors lay, coffin piled upon coffin, for ten generations together.

The place was so seldom visited that the rats had made free with the lead work, and now a thigh bone would catch at his cloak as he

---

[1] *Hydriotaphia*, London, 1929, p. 50.

passed, or he would crack the skull of some old Sir Malise as it rolled beneath his foot. It was a ghastly sepulchre; dug deep beneath the foundations of the house as if the first Lord of the family, who had come from France with the Conqueror, had wished to testify how all pomp is built upon corruption; how the skeleton lies beneath the flesh; how we that dance and sing above must lie below; how the crimson velvet turns to dust; how the ring (here Orlando, stooping his lantern, would pick up a gold circle lacking a stone, that had rolled into a corner) loses its ruby and the eye which was so lustrous shines no more.   (p. 67)

The crypt with the lead work destroyed by the rats, and with the thigh bone and skulls rolling about suggests death, decay and corruption. The destruction of the symbols of pomp, power, and glory—the crimson velvet turning to dust, the ring losing its ruby, and the eye its lustre—heightens the sense of the transitoriness of human life and glory.

Virginia Woolf feels that if an individual life, and even the glory of an age, is so transient, there is no reason for anyone to be proud of pomp and power. (This idea is dealt with again, as we shall see, in *Between the Acts*.) The absurdity of having 365 bedrooms which had been in the possession of the family for four or five hundred years, and of being proud of having earls, or even dukes as one's ancestors, is high-lighted by mentioning the simple gipsy whose family went back two or three thousand years, whose ancestors had built the Pyramids centuries before Christ was born, and who lived a life of 'making a basket' or 'skinning a sheep', and laughed at the 'vulgar ambition' of earls and dukes who snatch land or money from people and accumulate 'field after field; house after house; honour after honour' (p. 135–6).

Victoria Sackville-West was a novelist and a poet. She had won the Hawthornden Prize for her poem, *The Land*. Many of her ancestors were poets and writers. Orlando, reflecting their various talents, becomes a symbol of the literary traditions of the family. During the Elizabethan Age, like Thomas Sackville the first Earl of Dorset, who contributed to *Gorboduc* and *The Mirror of Magistrates*, he writes *Aethelbert: A Tragedy in Five Acts*; like Richard Sackville who was a friend and patron of Beaumont, Ben Jonson, Fletcher, and Drayton, he is a great lover of scholars. Victoria Sackville-West once offered hospitality to a poet, a friend of General Franco, who afterwards, according to Stephen Spender,[1] wrote against her; Orlando patronizes Mr. Nicholas Greene of Clifford's Inn, a poet, who in return for his hospitality writes 'a very spirited satire' about a visit to a nobleman in the country (p. 88). Nick Greene, the 'sardonic loose-lipped man' whose ridicule of Orlando's tragedy had not only hurt Orlando but also made him destroy his fifty-seven poetical works (p. 90), stands for the 'irresponsible' reviewer whose reviews affect the sensibility of authors.[2]

Ultimately Orlando swears, 'I'll write, from this day forward, to please myself' (p. 96), and indulges in profound thoughts as to the nature of obscurity (p. 97). In this he resembles his creator. 'I write,' Virginia Woolf says, 'what I like writing and there's an end on it.'[3] At another place she records, 'I'm the only woman in England free to write what I like,'[4] and she has described the advantages of 'obscurity' to a writer in *A Room of One's Own.*

Orlando, the writer, like Lily Briscoe, the artist in *To the Lighthouse*, and Miss La Trobe, the producer in *Between the Acts*, becomes a symbol of a creative artist, and reflects the 'rigours of composition'. He 'wrote and it seemed good; read and it seemed vile'; he alternated between ecstasy and despair, and wondered whether he was 'the divinest genius or the greatest fool' (p. 77), and these feelings, reflecting Virginia Woolf's own as we find them scattered throughout her diary, attain symbolic value.

In *Orlando* Virginia Woolf also portrays the successive ages of English life and letters, which she was to develop again in *The Years* and *Between the Acts*. Whereas in *Between the Acts* she describes them in a more terse and symbolic way through the pageant, in *Orlando* she is more explanatory, and uses atmosphere and seasons as symbols, a method that she was to employ again in *The Years*. About the Elizabethan Age in *Orlando* she says:

..... their morals were not ours; nor their poets; nor their climate; nor their vegetables even. Everything was different ..... Sunsets were redder and more intense; dawns were whiter and more auroral.

---

[1] *World Within World*, p. 152.
[2] Virginia Woolf, *Reviewing*, London, 1939, p. 7.
[3] *Diary*, p. 44.   [4] Ibid., p. 83.

Of our crepuscular half-lights and lingering twilights they knew
nothing ..... The sun rose and sank. The lover loved and went.
(pp. 27–28)

The redder and more intense sunsets symbolize the ardent
poets and the lovers of the 'garden flower' and of 'the wild and
the weeds', and the bold and free manners of men and women
who narrate 'how Jakes had lost his nose and Sukey her
honour' (p. 31).

One important result of the Augustan Age was to produce
a style of exemplary clarity, to write 'as Locke recommended
lucidly and without mystifying aura'.[1] Virginia Woolf describing the change in Orlando's style says,

His floridity was chastened; his abundance curbed; the age of prose
was congealing those warm fountains. The very landscape outside
was less stuck about with garlands and the briars themselves were
less thorned and intricate. Perhaps the senses were a little duller and
honey and cream less seductive to the palate.   (p. 104)

The duller scenes and senses, contrasting with the 'ingrained
habit of colour and passion' of the Elizabethans, become apt
symbols of the Age of Reason.

Similarly Virginia Woolf uses frost, the darkness of night,
clouds and dampness, and the clear and uniform skies, as
symbols to suggest the temper of an age, or the state of mind
of an individual. The Great Frost, when 'birds froze in mid-
air and fell like stones to the ground', not only provides an
occasion for Virginia Woolf to indulge in her flights of fantasy,
and a place for the escapades of Orlando and the revelries of the
new king, but also serves as a symbol of the callousness of the
court: 'while the country people suffered the extremity of
want', the capital, because the new king wanted to 'curry
favour with the citizens', enjoyed a carnival of utmost brilliancy.
The river, which had frozen, was 'to be swept, decorated and
given all the semblance of a park or pleasure ground' (p. 34).

The darkness and blackness, which Virginia Woolf mentions
fifteen times in six pages, and which make the night of 'so
inky a blackness that a man was on you before he could be
seen' (p. 55), creating a sinister atmosphere, becomes symbolic
of the deceit of Sasha, the Muscovite, and of the black mood of

[1] A. R. Humphreys, 'The Social Setting', *The Pelican Guide to English
Literature*, Vol. 4, p. 43.

Orlando, the cheated. When 'with an awful and ominous voice, a voice full of horror and alarm' (p. 57), St. Paul's struck the stroke of midnight, Orlando, standing in the doorway of an inn near Blackfriars, knew that his doom was sealed.

> He stood in the doorway in the tremendous rain without moving. As the minutes passed, he sagged a little at the knees. The downpour rushed on. In the thick of it, great guns seemed to boom. Huge noises as of the tearing and rending of oak trees could be heard. There were also wild cries and terrible inhuman groanings.
>
> (pp. 57–58)

The 'huge noises' and the 'wild cries' and 'inhuman groanings', symbolize the lacerating of Orlando's heart and his anguished cry at being cheated by Sasha. Similarly the 'turbulent yellow waters', the mere look of which was 'enough to turn one giddy', which Orlando saw instead of 'the solid ice' the river had been for three months, become symbols of the riot and confusion of his mind (p. 58).

When he saw the ship of the Muscovite Embassy standing out to sea, Orlando flung himself from his horse, and in his rage tried to breast the sea:

> he hurled at the faithless woman all the insults that have ever been the lot of her sex. Faithless, mutable, fickle, he called her; devil, adulteress, deceiver; and the swirling waters took his words, and tossed at his feet a broken pot and a little straw.   (p. 61)

The broken pot and the little straw, remnants of a wrecked home and a nest destroyed, that the sea tossed at his feet, become symbols of his shattered dreams of a comfortable home that he wanted to found with Sasha.

After describing how Orlando met Pope, Addison, Swift, and Lord Chesterfield, and saw Dr. Johnson, Mr. Boswell, and Mrs. Williams, Virginia Woolf closes the chapter with a description of the spreading clouds.

At length she came home one night after one of these saunterings ..... and stood there ..... looking out of the window ..... She could see St. Paul's, the Tower, Westminster Abbey, with all the spires and domes of the city churches ..... Upon this serene and orderly prospect the stars looked down, glittering, positive, hard, from a cloudless sky. In the extreme clearness of the atmosphere the line of every roof, the cowl of every chimney was perceptible ..... She heard the far-away cry of the night watchman—'Just twelve o'clock on a frosty morning'. No sooner had the words left his lips than the first stroke of midnight sounded. Orlando then for the first time noticed a small cloud gathered behind the dome of St. Paul's. As the strokes sounded, the cloud increased and she saw it darken and spread with extraordinary speed ..... With the twelfth stroke of midnight, the darkness was complete. A turbulent welter of cloud covered the city. All was darkness; all was doubt; all was confusion. The Eighteenth century was over; the Nineteenth century had begun.

(pp. 202–4)

'The extreme clearness of the atmosphere', the 'cloudless sky', the 'glittering, positive, hard' stars, and the 'orderly prospect', evoking the lucid style and the extreme rationalism of Addison, Pope, and Swift, become symbolic of the Age of Reason. Similarly the spreading clouds, and the 'doubt' and 'confusion' symbolize Romanticism and the Victorian Age, which had, as Lytton Strachey says, 'barbarism and prudery',[1] and 'self-complacency and self-contradiction'.[2] Virginia Woolf further expresses her ideas about the Victorian Age by using the ever increasing dampness and ivy as symbols.

But what was worse, damp now began to make its way into every house—damp, which is the most insidious of all enemies, for while the sun can be shut out by blinds, and the frost roasted by a hot fire, damp steals in while we sleep; damp is silent, imperceptible, ubiquitous. Damp swells the wood, furs the kettle, rusts the iron, rots the stone.   (p. 205)

This dampness makes men feel 'the chill in their hearts; the damp in their mind'. This condition of the moral and mental state of the Victorians is taken up again and dealt with exhaustively in *The Years* and *Three Guineas*. The dampness makes ivy grow in 'unparalleled profusion'. It smothers the bare stones of the houses in greenery. This concealing of even the bare stones by the ivy suggests the 'evasions and concealments' that were sedulously practised by both the sexes, and the prudery of the Victorian Age. The dampness not only makes ivy grow, but also makes vegetation become 'rampant'. Cucumbers 'came scrolloping across the grass', and 'giant cauliflowers' tower deck

---

[1] *Portraits in Miniature*, London, 1931, p. 193.
[2] *Characters and Commentaries*, London, 1933, p. 231.

above deck. This 'fecundity of the garden, the bedroom and the henroost' (p. 208) becomes symbolic of the large Victorian families. This fecundity, which is the spirit of the age, is expressed when Orlando, now wearing a crinoline and a plumed hat in the Victorian fashion, wants someone to 'lean upon' (p. 222).

The cloudy sky, that had engendered dampness and ivy, bearded men, and even muffled furniture, changes with the changing eras.

It was no longer so thick, so watery, so prismatic now that King Edward ..... had succeeded Queen Victoria. The clouds had shrunk to a thin gauze; the sky seemed made of metal, which in hot weather tarnished ..... It was a little alarming—this shrinkage. Everything seemed to have shrunk.   (pp. 266–7)

This shrinkage in King Edward's time is symbolic of the change that took place in the dress, manners, and tastes of the age. The dresses became short and less cumbersome, women grew narrow 'like stalks of corn, straight, shining, identical'. Men's faces became 'bare as the palm of one's hand'. The curtains and covers became frizzled up and the walls became bare to be decorated by 'brilliant coloured pictures of real things'. The families, coming within the grip of shrinkage, also ceased to grow large (pp. 267–8).

In spite of the fact that Virginia Woolf did not have good health and being very sensitive was depressed by the inhuman wars, she was, Clive Bell records, 'the gayest human being',[1] and she saw 'life itself as a vast Shakespearean Comedy'.[2] Thus she is able to create delightful comedies in *Orlando* and *Between the Acts*, to see the brighter side of life, and believe in progress. Her last two novels, even though they were written under the shadow of war, show the same spirit of hope and progress. This spirit is symbolized in *The Years* through the young couple and the rising dawn, and in *Between the Acts* through the birth of a new life and the raising of the curtain for a new play. In *Orlando* it is expressed through another symbol:

..... as she was thinking this, the immensely long tunnel in which she seemed to have been travelling for hundreds of years widened; the

[1] *Old Friends*, London, 1956, p. 99.
[2] David Garnett, *The Flowers of the Forest*, London, 1955, p. 161.

light poured in ..... And so for some seconds the light went on becoming brighter and brighter, and she saw everything more and more clearly and the clock ticked louder and louder until there was a terrific explosion right in her ear ..... Ten times she was struck. In fact it was ten o'clock in the morning. It was the eleventh of October. It was 1928. It was the present time.   (p. 268)

The long tunnel stands for time. The light becoming brighter as the end—the present time—approaches is a symbol of Virginia Woolf's delight in the progress the world has made. This is both material progress—from the muffled overcrowded Victorian houses with their 'small tin bath tubs'[1] to the sanitary and convenient modern houses with their shower baths, from travelling 'for hours with one's feet in dirty straw dragged along the streets by horses' to riding in omnibuses and motor-cars— and also the progress towards mental and spiritual freedom, for Orlando, in contrast to the mothers and unpaid house-keepers of the previous age, is now free to write poetry and win prizes, and to be her own mistress.

As Virginia Woolf calls *Orlando* a biography, she also presents in it symbolically her ideas about the art of biography. She seems to believe with Lytton Strachey and Victoria Sackville-West, that the function of a biographer is to be truthful. Desmond MacCarthy sums up Lytton Strachey's ideal about the art of biography in the following words:

..... biography must aim at being a truthful record of an individual life, composed as a work of art.[2]

Victoria Sackville-West feels that to write a biography is not 'to write a panegyric'.[3] Virginia Woolf symbolically expresses these ideas through Our Ladies of Purity, Chastity, and Modesty. Like De Quincey's Ladies of Sorrow who address a new born child,[4] they address the newly changed Orlando. These Ladies, who 'cover vice and poverty', and all those things that are 'frail or dark or doubtful', saying 'speak not, reveal not', and who hide behind 'ivy and curtains', sing in unison thus:

Truth come not out from your horrid den. Hide deeper, fearful Truth. For you flaunt in the brutal gaze of the sun things that were

---

[1] Lytton Strachey, *Portraits in Miniature*, p. 193.
[2] *Memories*, London, 1953, p. 32.   [3] *Pepita*, London, 1937, p. 282.
[4] *De Quincey's Works*, Vol. XIII, Edinburgh, 1890, p. 365.

better unknown and undone; you unveil the shameful; the dark you make clear, Hide! Hide! Hide!   (pp. 124–5)

This exhortation of theirs that Truth should hide rather than unveil the shameful makes them symbolic of that school of biographers who mention only 'those performances and incidents which produce vulgar greatness' and who, thinking it 'an act of piety', try to hide the faults and failings of the men they portray by not leading the thoughts into their 'domestic privacies' and the 'minutest details' of their private lives.

CHAPTER SEVEN

The Waves

A STUDY of Virginia Woolf's diary reveals that she considered *The Waves* to be her most mystical book. It was to be, as she says, 'an abstract mystical eyeless book' in which she had to come to terms with her 'mystical feelings',[1] and to say 'certain things' that she had meant to say.[2] In this 'very mystical poetical work', which Baudelaire would call 'la nouvelle poétique', she has tried to net 'that fin in the waste of water' which had appeared to her over the marshes out of her window at Rodmell.[3]

What the vision at Rodmell meant, and what the thoughts and feelings that she was trying to embody were, she has described more fully elsewhere in her diary:

I wished to add some remarks to this, on the mystical side of this solicitude; how it is not oneself but something in the universe that one's left with. It is this that is frightening and exciting in the midst of my profound gloom, depression, boredom, whatever it is. One sees a fin passing far out. What image can I reach to convey what I mean? Really there is none, I think. The interesting thing is that in all my feeling and thinking I have never come up against this before. Life is, soberly and accurately, the oddest affair; has in it the essence of reality.[4]

What exactly she means by reality she has explained at another place:

Often down here I have entered into a sanctuary; a nunnery; had a religious retreat; of great agony once; and always some terror; so afraid one is of loneliness; of seeing to the bottom of the vessel. That is one of the experiences I have had here in some Augusts; and got then to a consciousness of what I call 'reality': a thing I see before me: something abstract; but residing in the downs or sky;

---

[1] *Diary*, p. 137.   [2] Ibid., p. 167.   [3] Ibid., p.169.
[4] Ibid., p. 101.

H

beside which nothing matters; in which I shall rest and continue to exist. Reality I call it. And I fancy sometimes this is the most necessary thing to me: that which I seek.[1]

These two entries from her most intimate writing, which are not the outcome of some flippant mood but are the result of illumination—matches struck in darkness, as Virginia Woolf would have put it—gained during such intense moments as one at times experiences in a 'sanctuary' during a 'religious retreat', make it explicit that Virginia Woolf thinks that 'reality' is something abstract, and that life, which has the essence of reality, will rest in it and thus continue to exist. In this context Virginia Woolf means by 'life' something similar to what Clarissa in *Mrs. Dalloway* meant about her life when she thought that her body 'with all its capacities' was nothing, and that she was 'herself invisible; unseen; unknown .....' i.e. the 'blissful thing' that, according to Vaughan, 'doeth vivifie', and which, in contradistinction to body, is known as spirit—the indwelling vivifying essence.

Before Virginia Woolf attained the age of twenty-five, she had witnessed the deaths of her maternal and paternal grandparents, of Stella, her step-sister, and of her mother, father, and brother. The deaths of her mother, father, and brother affected her so much that she suffered nervous breakdowns as a result. Even though, having seen these deaths in the family during the tender and formative years of her life, and later having seen the mowing down of lives in the First World War, Virginia Woolf had become acutely conscious of the transitoriness of human life, whose flux and incessant change she has masterfully depicted in memorable passages of prose scattered throughout her novels, yet she does not seem to believe that 'Naught may endure but Mutability'. On the contrary she questioned herself whether life is 'very solid or very shifting'. And her thoughts about passing 'like cloud on the wave' are usually accompanied by reflections 'that though we change, one flying after another, so quick, so quick, yet we are somehow successive and continuous .....'

This seeming contradiction between the flux, mutability, and the ever becoming of life, and the fixity, constancy, and

---

[1] *Diary*, p. 132.

being of reality, Virginia Woolf has resolved artistically, if not philosophically, in *The Waves* by skilfully employing the waves and the sea as appropriate symbols of life and reality. Just as ripples rise out of the sea, grow into separate waves, rise higher and bigger, then break and subside into the sea becoming part of it again, in the same manner human beings take birth as different individuals, like Bernard, Neville, Louis, Susan, Jinny, and Rhoda, and passing through infancy, youth, and old age, ultimately rest in reality, and there, achieving 'fusion with the eternal spiritual principal', continue to exist. This is similar to an idea expressed by Maulana Rumi, a Persian mystic, in his *Masnavi-i-Ma'navi*, which in E. H. Whinfield's translation reads:

> When waves of thought arise from the Ocean of Wisdom,
> They assume the forms of sound and speech.
> These forms of speech are born and die again,
> These waves cast themselves back into the Ocean.
> Form is born of That which is without form,
> And goes again, for, 'Verily to Him do we return.'[1]

This is Virginia Woolf's vision of life and reality. Both this vision and the symbols that she employs to evoke it are archetypal, because since remotest times the saints and sages have had similar visions, and the *vates* and the modern psychologists have employed and explained identical symbols. A comparison between some of the quotations from her diary given above and the sayings of mystics and the beliefs of sages will bring out their inherent similarity.

Being the daughter of an agnostic, and the possessor of an inquiring mind, Virginia Woolf could not see reality in terms of theistic symbols. She could not see it as the Christian Trinity or Hindu Trimurti, simply because, unlike the Christian saints or the Oriental devotees, Virginia Woolf was not an adherent of any institutional religion. Therefore she saw reality as 'something abstract', like Shelley's 'An awful shadow of some unseen power'. The Lord Buddha, explaining that the Immeasurable and the Fathomless can neither be seen nor explained, says,

[1] Op. cit., London, 1887, p. 24.

OM, AMITAYA! measure not with words
   Th' Immeasurable; nor sink the string of thought
Into the Fathomless. Who asks doeth err,
   Who answers, errs. Say naught!

     .....

Shall any gazer see with mortal eyes,
   Or any searcher know by mortal mind,
Veil after veil will lift—but there must be
   Veil upon veil behind.[1]

So Virginia Woolf, too, in the modern terminology of motor-cars has expressed the limitations of the mortal mind to see the Invisible Light, that, according to T. S. Eliot in 'The Rock', is 'Too bright for mortal vision'. 'At night L. and I talked of death again', she writes in her diary, 'the second time this year: how we may be like worms crushed by a motor car: what does the worm know of the car—how it is made? There may be a reason: if so not one we, as human beings, can grasp.'[2] Like the worm crushed under a motor-car, mortal minds have their limitations. Reality to such minds can only be some awful abstract power.

This abstract power, which Wordsworth in 'The Prelude' names 'An active Principle', subsists in all things, in all natures, permeates everything and pervades everywhere. Dante expresses this idea in 'Paradiso' where he says,

His Glory, all things moving, motionless,
   Spreads through the universe, and more reglows
In one fair part and in another less.

T. S. Eliot, also, has expressed a similar idea in 'The Dry Salvages' when he says, 'The river is within us, the sea is all about us.' It is something like this that Virginia Woolf means when she says that she sees reality 'residing in the down or sky', and when she asserts that life 'has in it the essence of reality'. Because Virginia Woolf, unlike the saints and mystics, had not trodden the mystic way of 'purification, illumination, and union', as described by Dionysius the Areopagite, nor undergone disciplined meditation, she could not express her vaguely

---

[1] Sir Edwin Arnold, *The Light of Asia*, London, 1926, p. 158.
[2] *Diary*, p. 184.

felt vision in the more positive way of the seer of the *Chhāndôgya-Upanishad*, of Farid-ud Din Attar, the Persian mystic, or of St. John of the Cross and St. Teresa the Christian saints. In order to make Shwetaketu, an individualized human soul, conscious of his inherent dignity and glory, Uddālaka in the *Chhāndôgya-Upanishad* teaches him thus: 'That Being is the seed; all else but His expression. He is truth, He is Self. Shwetaketu! You are That.'[1] The Persian mystic in his allegorical epic, *The Conversation of the Birds*, clearly brings out this point that life not merely has the essence of, but is in essence reality. When the thirty birds, who have set out in quest of the Divine Bird—the Simurg—on reaching his court lifted up their eyes to see him, they

> Beheld the Figure of—*Themselves*—as't were
> Transfigured—looking to Themselves, beheld
> The Figure on the Throne en-miracled,
> Until their Eyes themselves and *That* between
> Did hesitate which *Seer* was, which *Seen*;
> They that, that they: Another, yet the Same;
> Dividual, yet One.[2]

Thus it can be safely inferred from this comparative study that Virginia Woolf is thinking in the traditional mystical way when she says that reality is something abstract, and that it pervades everywhere residing in the downs as well as the sky.

The next assertion that she makes, that she shall 'rest and continue to exist' in reality, sounds, too, like an echo of the Persian mystic's faith about 'Fana' and 'Baqa'—to die into God and to abide in and with Him. This is also in keeping with the mystical tradition. The Lord Buddha, describing the ultimate stage of a human being, says,

> He goes
> Unto NIRVANA. He is one with life
> Yet lives not. He is blest, ceasing to be.
> OM, MANI PADME, OM! The Dewdrop slips
> Into the Shining Sea![3]

[1] Shree Purohit Swāmi and W. B. Yeats, *The Ten Principal Upanishads*, London, 1938, p. 91.
[2] A. J. Arberry, *Sufism*, London, 1950, p. 108.
[3] Sir Edwin Arnold, *The Light of Asia*, p. 166.

The dewdrop, like the breaking waves, slips into the sea, rests there, and continues to exist there. For him the struggle and restlessness of life is over, and change and flux cease. For him death is not annihilation. It is resurrection, and that, too, into a greater and more glorious life. That Virginia Woolf felt something like this is clear from what Victoria Sackville-West says about her, and from the peroration of Bernard to death in *The Waves*. Victoria Sackville-West writes:

..... but what I remember most vividly is one night when a superb thunderstorm broke over Vezelay and we sat in darkness while the flashes intermittently lit up her face. She was, I think, a little frightened, and perhaps that drove her to speak, with a deeper seriousness than I had ever heard her use before, of immortality and personal survival after death.[1]

Addressing Death, Bernard says,

And in me too the wave rises. It swells; it arches its back. I am aware once more of a new desire, something rising beneath me like the proud horse whose rider first spurs then pulls him back. What enemy do we now perceive advancing against us, you whom I ride now, as we stand pawing this stretch of pavement? It is death. Death is the enemy. It is death against whom I ride with my spear couched and my hair flying back like a young man's, like Percival's, when he galloped in India. I strike spurs into my horse. Against you I will fling myself, unvanquished and unyielding, O Death.

(*The Waves*, p. 211)

Like the Knights of the Holy Grail, Bernard charges against death, and remains unvanquished, because when one realizes that by residing in reality one continues to exist, Death as a leveller and annihilator ceases to be. Clarissa in *Mrs. Dalloway*, and Mrs. Ramsay in *To the Lighthouse*, had also felt this truth vaguely. They were groping after what Bernard understood and expressed about survival after death, about continuance of life.

Life, like the waves that rising out of the sea again subside into it, emerges out of and then submerges into reality. So the sea, composed of water, the 'prima materia' of the English alchemist George Ripley, is a self-explanatory symbol of reality. This symbol has also been employed by St. Teresa, who, writing about spiritual marriage, says,

[1] 'Notes on Virginia Woolf', *Horizon*, Vol. III, No. 17, May 1941, p. 322.

But spiritual marriage is like rain falling from heaven into a river or stream, becoming one and the same liquid, so that the river and rain water cannot be divided; or it resembles a streamlet flowing into the ocean, which cannot afterwards be disunited from it.[1]

As already shown earlier both T. S. Eliot and the Lord Buddha have employed the sea as a symbol of the Vast Unknown. As the sea is a multi-faceted symbol Virginia Woolf, besides employing it mystically as a symbol of reality, also uses it psychologically to suggest the collective unconscious. A wave in that case becomes a symbol of an individual 'self'.

Bernard, Neville, Louis, Susan, Jinny, and Rhoda in *The Waves* are different personalities representing various types of characters. The opening sentences that they utter as young children, like the dream language, symbolize their innate personalities which flower with them into their typical characters. They are not, as Philip Toynbee says, 'perfectly interchangeable', nor devoid of 'clear symbolic differentiation'.[2] 'I see a ring', said Bernard, 'hanging above me. It quivers and hangs in a loop of light.' This saying of Bernard's is like the ecstatic cry of the mystic poet, Vaughan, who says,

> I saw Eternity the other night
> Like a great *Ring* of pure and endless light.

It is also like the 'round gold ring' and 'the Ring of Recurrrence' of Nietzsche.[3] It resembles the 'opus circulare' of the alchemists which is sometimes represented as Uroboros—the dragon biting its own tail. Just as the golden ring represented to Nietzsche 'a promise of resurrection and life', and the 'opus circulare' to the Alchemists meant proceeding from the one and leading back to the one, the ring hanging in a loop of light that Bernard sees symbolizes a mystic vision of reality, of the 'eternal renewal' (p. 211), which he often proclaims when he says 'The circle is unbroken; the harmony complete' (p. 68).

Whereas Bernard is an intuitive and a mystic, Neville is an intellectual. As Bernard says, he indulges in no mystification

---

[1] *The Interior Castle*, London, 1901, p. 272.
[2] 'Virginia Woolf, A Study of Three Experimental Novels', *Horizon*, Vol. XIV, No. 83, November, 1946, p. 294.
[3] *Thus Spake Zarathustra, The Philosophy of Nietzsche*, N.Y., 1937, pp. 204, 244.

(p. 61). He is a man with clarity of intelligence and honesty of intellect. Like Mr. Ramsay who is 'lean as a knife, narrow as the blade of one', Neville is 'scissor-cutting, exact' (p. 84), and his knife, like the knife of Peter in *Mrs. Dalloway*, becomes a symbol of his intellect. Of all the characters in *The Waves* he alone is delicate. He easily gets tired and then is sick (p. 17). This delicate health is also symbolic. It represents what St. Paul says about wisdom: 'that by wisdom no man ever arrived at knowledge of God', i.e. the inherent inability of intellect to comprehend reality. Not having attained the knowledge of God, Neville becomes intolerant and contemptuous. He denounces the 'piffling, trifling, self-satisfied world' with its smugness and mediocrity (p. 51). About his contemptuous nature he himself says, 'I am already at eighteen capable of such contempt that horse-breeders hate me' (p. 51). Unlike Mrs. Ramsay who, having glimpsed truth and reality, is aglow and beautiful, Neville, not having had an intuition of beauty, remains ugly (p. 129). His scissor-cutting mind which is like an 'astonishing rapier' (p. 65) desires order, and detests Byronic untidiness. Not being able, like Bernard, to see 'the unmoving Mover' behind the movement of life, Neville wants to feel 'the crystal, the globe of life' (p. 182) to be hard and cold to the touch. His first words about seeing 'a globe' (p. 6), therefore, attain symbolic value too. In *Jacob's Room* (p. 91), and *Night and Day* (p. 533) Virginia Woolf has already used 'globe' as an image for perfected life which one tries to shape 'round, whole, and entire from the confusion of chaos'.

Louis is neither a mystic nor an intellectual. He is all the time conscious of his Australian accent and that his father is a banker in Brisbane (p. 14). This gives him an inferiority complex and colours his whole character. He wants to be like Bernard and Neville who are sons of gentlemen (p. 14). He tries to imitate them because he wants to be 'they' (p. 26). When he feels that in spite of his knowing 'more than they will ever know' (p. 14), and being the 'best scholar in the school' (p. 38), the difference has not been solved, he feels bitter (p. 42). On leaving school he feels that he has 'no firm ground' to step on. 'Bernard and Neville, Percival, Archie, Larpent and Baker' he says, 'go to Oxford or Cambridge, to Edinburgh, Rome, Paris, Berlin, or to some American University. I go vaguely, to make money vaguely' (p. 47). Then, comparing his future with theirs, he says:

They are all boasting, all talking ..... and so will always slip into cushioned firelit rooms, with many books and one friend, while I tilt on an office chair behind a counter. Then I shall grow bitter and mock at them. I shall envy them their continuance down the safe traditional ways under the shade of old yew trees while I consort with cockneys and clerks, and tap the pavements of the city.

(p. 48)

This makes him feel indignant, 'and impulses wilder than the wildest birds' strike from his wild heart (p. 42). Being unable to break away from his past, he feels like a chained beast, 'a caged tiger' (p. 92). But he wants to break those chains and smash those bars. He wants to compensate for his Australian accent and for his father being a banker. He hopes to inherit an arm-chair and a Turkey carpet (p. 119). Therefore his first utterance, 'I hear something stamping. A great beast's foot is chained. It stamps, and stamps, and stamps' (p. 6), suggesting his characteristic leanings to break free and push forward, attains symbolic value.

Similarly Susan, Jinny, and Rhoda, who also represent different types of personalities, use words symbolic of their inborn tendencies. Susan, like the Greek men and women in *Jacob's Room*, does not want to live an emasculated life. She is elemental. She is not 'afraid of the heat, or of the frozen winter' (p. 18). She wants natural life and natural happiness (p. 94). Therefore the sayings that she understands best 'are cries of love, hate, rage and pain' (p. 94). What she likes best is 'the stare of shepherds met in the road; the stare of gipsy women beside a cart in a ditch suckling their children' (p. 71), as she will suckle her children, and thus enjoy 'the bestial and beautiful passion of maternity' (p. 94). She hates sophistication. She hates school, for she thinks that in school there all 'is false; all is meretricious' (p. 23), and that 'at school in Switzerland, some hard thing' had formed in her side. Therefore she says, 'I will not send my children to school nor spend a night all my life in London' (p. 44). For she feels that in London everything 'echoes and booms hollowly' (p. 45). The words 'I love and I hate' that she repeats are symbolic of her elemental nature which feels 'glutted with natural happiness' as she croons her baby to sleep and thinks, 'Yet more will come, more children; more cradles, more baskets in the kitchen and hams ripening; and onions glistening; and more beds of lettuce and potatoes' (p. 123). This elemental creature who has 'the yellow warmth' in her side and who is 'storm-tinted and all one purple' (pp. 10, 94), expresses her character symbolically in her first remark: 'I see a slab of pale yellow ..... spreading away until it meets a purple stripe' (p. 6).

'I see a crimson tassel twisted with gold thread' are Jinny's opening words, and they epitomize her character. Unlike Susan who is elemental and solid, Jinny is a 'feather-headed' creature (p. 40). for whom there is 'nothing staid, nothing settled, in the universe' (p. 33). She is restless and has no peace of mind, no tranquillity. This is symbolized by her rippling, dancing (p. 9), by her leaping 'like one of those flames that run' between the cracks of the earth' (p. 30), and by her ever 'pirouetting' (p. 40). She is all body and no soul. Her body lives a life of its own (p. 45), in 'the great society of bodies' (p. 46). She can imagine nothing beyond the circle cast by her body (p. 92). 'Our bodies communicate', she says. 'This is my calling' (p. 73). She is conscious of the 'heat and rapture' that bodies communicate (p. 46). Having this religion of the body, she wants to decorate and worship it. Conscious of the heat of her body, she thinks in terms of glowing heat and fire. 'I should like a fiery dress,' she says, 'a yellow dress, a fulvous dress to wear in the evening' (p. 15). She also wants to have a 'thin dress shot with red threads that would gleam in the firelight' (p. 24). Jinny dancing like a flame, febrile, hot ..... (p. 84) is, as Bernard sums her up, 'honest, an animal'. True to her animality and the calling of the body, she trembles and quivers with passion. When someone finding in her 'some quality, some peculiar thing' is attracted towards her, she will not let herself be attached to one person only, because, as she says, she does not want 'to be fixed, to be pinioned' (p. 40). Even when she is no longer young, she does not give up. She marches forward. She powders her face and reddens her lips. She makes the angles of her brow sharper than usual. She decorates her room and waits for 'somebody new, somebody unknown', for somebody she had passed on a staircase and to whom she had murmured,

'Come' (p. 139). This 'little animal', as she calls herself (p. 137). a palpitating trembling body, whose very 'imagination is the body's' (p. 156), naturally thinks of a crimson tassel with gold thread.

Rhoda, like Louis, is timid. That is why, like Louis, and unlike the other four who 'see', she 'hears' something. Whereas Louis hears the more masculine stamping of a chained beast, Rhoda hears a feminine 'cheep, chirp; cheep, chirp' of a solitary bird that 'sings by the bedroom window alone' (pp. 6, 7). Louis who was prepared to consort with cockneys and clerks, not only faces life boldly, but also is able to fight against it successfully, thus ensuring for himself a place in Surrey. Being more timid than he, Rhoda cannot face life. Life for her is an 'emerging monster'. With intermittent shocks, sudden as the spring of a tiger, it emerges 'heaving its dark crest from the sea' (p. 47). Every time that she comes across life, fear grips her. 'The door opens; terror rushes in; terror upon terror pursuing me', she says (p. 75). 'The door opens and the tiger leaps', she says again (p. 93). She is afraid of being 'knocked against and damaged' by hard contacts and collisions. That is why she cries, 'Hide me, I cry, protect me .....' Being unable to mix with people, to face life, she always tries to hide behind people (p. 30), or, to be away from activity, she longs for night to be able to drift into her dream world, to lie suspended on her bed above the world (p. 40). She is a dreamer, and is conscious of her thin and papery dreams (p. 41). This imaginative and romantic creature—'the nymph of the fountain always wet' (p. 84)—who dreads life and hates human beings (p. 145), cannot establish human contacts. 'To whom shall I give all that now flows through me,' she says, 'from my warm, my porous body? I will gather my flowers and present them—Oh! to whom?' (p. 41). This is her tragedy. Her life is all dreams and has no contact with life, no action. Therefore, she feels that she is 'alone in a hostile world' (p. 113). The cheep, chirp, cheep, chirp, of a bird singing by the bedroom window alone, becomes a symbol of her timid character.

The infancy, childhood, youth, and old age of these personalities are treated in different sections of *The Waves*. The lyrical sections preceding these are in an intense poetic language. Like the choruses in a play or the intermezzos of an opera, they not only connect up the various parts, but also explain what follows in the succeeding sections. Virginia Woolf had felt the necessity of introducing these interludes in order to giver her book the right shape. 'But how to pull it together,' she writes in her diary, 'how to comport it—press it into one ..... The interludes are very difficult, yet I think essential; so as to bridge and also to give a background—the sea; insensitive nature .....'[1] These, which Joan Bennett calls overcharged 'descriptive interludes',[2] are in themselves beautiful pieces of literature that paint in words vivid sea- and land-scapes. The book opens with the following words:

The sun had not yet risen. The sea was indistinguishable from the sky, except that the sea was slightly creased as if a cloth had wrinkles in it. Gradually as the sky whitened a dark line lay on the horizon dividing the sea from the sky and the grey cloth became barred with thick strokes moving, one after another, beneath the surface, follow- ing each other, pursuing each other, perpetually .....

   Gradually the dark bar on the horizon became clear ..... Behind it, too, the sky cleared ..... as if the arm of a woman couched beneath the horizon had raised a lamp ..... Slowly the arm that held the lamp raised it higher and then higher until a broad flame became visible, an arc of fire burnt on the rim of the horizon, and all round it the sea blazed gold.

   The light struck upon the trees in the garden, making one leaf transparent and then another. One bird chirped higher up; there was a pause; another chirped lower down. The sun sharpened the walls of the house ..... The blind stirred slightly, but all within was dim and unsubstantial. The birds sang their blank melody outside.   (pp. 5–6)

The first section of *The Waves*, following this interlude, deals with the infancy of the six characters and their time at a kinder- garten. Unlike adults or older boys and girls, these young children are not acutely conscious of their feelings or thoughts, nor are their actions and pranks motivated by set purposes. Virginia Woolf, therefore, in this interlude employs the traditional symbols of the sea, sun, house, and birds to evoke a relevant atmosphere. The sun has just risen, the waves on the sea are only small bars, and though the outer walls of the house have become sharpened, yet, like the indistinct feelings

---

[1] *Diary*, p. 153.   [2] Op. cit., p. 105.

and sensations of the children, the interior of the house is still 'dim and unsubstantial'. The birds have started singing, but their melody, too, is still 'blank'.

When the children grow up, they start acquiring distinct personalities. From the kindergarten they move to other schools, the boys to one, and girls to another. 'The birds, whose breasts were specked canary and rose, now sang a strain or two, together, wildly, like skaters rollicking arm-in-arm, and were suddenly silent, breaking asunder' (p. 20). The sun also rising a little higher 'sharpened the edges of chairs and tables' (p. 21). Thus, as the feelings and thoughts of the characters become more pronounced, the interior of the house, representing their minds, and the things in it, standing for their thoughts and emotions, become clearly outlined. But because they have not yet grown into men and women with defined passions and egotistical thoughts, everything in the house, though visible, is still 'softly amorphous' (p. 21).

When the characters in *The Waves* become full-grown individuals conscious of pleasure and pain, desire and hunger, and when they acquire the 'sensibility of a woman' or the 'logical sobriety of a man' with 'the double capacity to feel, to reason' (p. 55), and when they become reflective (p. 56), and conscious of their selves (p. 57), the birds in the interlude also undergo a comparable change.

In the garden the birds that had sung erratically and spasmodically in the dawn on that tree, on that bush, now sang together in chorus, shrill and sharp; now together, as if conscious of companionship, now alone as if to the pale blue sky. They swerved all in one flight, when the black cat moved among the bushes, when the cook threw cinders on the ash heap and startled them. Fear was in their song, and apprehension of pain, and joy to be snatched quickly now at this instant. Also they sang emulously in the clear morning air, swerving high over the elm tree, singing together as they chased each other, escaping, pursuing, pecking each other as they turned high in the air. And then tiring of pursuit and flight, lovelily they came descending, delicately declining, dropped down and sat silent on the tree, on the wall, with their bright eyes glancing, and their heads turned this way, that way; aware, awake; intensely conscious of one thing, one object in particular.   (p. 53)

The birds in this interlude, like the reflective and conscious selves of the characters, become 'aware, awake'; and there is in their song fear and apprehension of pain.

The waves, which symbolize the individual consciousnesses, also grow bigger. They mass themselves, their green hollows deepen and darken (p. 53). Similarly the interior of the house, too, becomes more marked, its 'circles and lines' become more distinct (p. 54).

In the same manner the development of the characters in the subsequent sections has a symbolic echo in the relevant interludes. In one interlude she says,

In the garden where the tree stood thick over flower-beds, ponds, and greenhouses the birds sang in the hot sunshine, each alone. One sang under the bedroom window; another on the topmost twig of the lilac bush; another on the edge of the wall. Each sang stridently, with passion, with vehemence, as if to let the song burst out of it, no matter if it shattered the song of another bird with harsh discord.

(p. 78)

As the birds in this interlude sing 'each alone', the people in the subsequent section assert their individuality and go their separate ways. Seeing the people following different ways, Bernard remarks, 'They are off. They are all impelled by some necessity. Some miserable affair of keeping an appointment, of buying a hat, severs these beautiful human beings once so united' (p. 81). And Susan says, 'I shall push the fortunes of my children unscrupulously. I shall hate those who see their faults. I shall lie basely to help them. I shall let them wall me away from you, from you and from you' (pp. 94–95). This declaration echoes the idea expressed in 'Each sang stridently, with passion ..... no matter if it shattered the song of another bird with harsh discord'. Similarly, as the characters attain cut-and-dried individualities, the interior of the house attains a hardness of shape in the 'sharp-edged wedges of light', and the things inside it appear in a more distinct outline showing their blue rings, curved handles, criss-cross patterns, and formidable corners and lines (p. 107).

In the last interlude, in keeping with what Bernard says about the summing up and the meaning of life (p. 168), about his not knowing whether he is a man or a woman (p. 199), and about our existing in undifferentiated blobs of matter (p. 174), the interior of the house once again loses its sharp edges, and the cupboards and chairs melt 'their brown masses into one huge obscurity', till the waves of darkness rolling in cover everything (pp. 167–8).

Similarly, according to the infancy, childhood, youth, and old age of the characters in *The Waves*, the sun in the various interludes occupies an appropriate position on its diurnal course. The sun, thus, becomes a symbol of age. And, as its position in the sky parallels the lucidity of the thoughts and feelings of the characters which progress in the same degree of distinctness as things receive from the light of the sun, it also becomes a symbol of intellect.

In the finale of this symphonic poem Bernard, while summing up his life and Virginia Woolf's vision of life and reality, employs many more original symbols. He tries to sum up life comprehensively in all its aspects, physical, psychological, and spiritual: the *Khat*, *Kha*, and *Khou* of the Egyptians.[1] In its physical and material aspect life is what we see lived every day by different people of diverse ages engaged in various occupations. In the psychological sense it is the inner life of the individual as a total personality, including both the conscious ego and the unconscious mind with all its thinking and feeling, with all its libidinal drives. Lastly, on its spiritual level, life is the unknown uncircumscribed spirit, the vivifying factor that makes the body live, the essence of reality. This dome of many coloured glass—'life'—as Bernard says, 'is not susceptible perhaps to the treatment we give it when we try to tell it' (p. 189). It is not solid with a neat design like a crystal or a globe hard and cold to the touch, nor is it like 'a bunch of grapes' which Bernard could break off and hand entire saying, 'Take it. This is my life.' On the contrary, life defies neat designs. That is why in order to explain his life Bernard longs for 'some little language such as lovers use, broken words, inarticulate words, like the shuffling of feet on the pavement' (p. 169). He needs 'words of one syllable such as children speak ..... a howl; a cry' (p. 209). To convey the meaning and the complexity of life, therefore, he needs symbols.

[1] Papus (Dr. G. Encausse), *Reincarnation*, London, n.d., p. 32. He reports that, according to the Egyptians, the incarnate man consisted of a body, *Khat*; an astral double, *Kha*; and a spirit, *Khou*.

In order to suggest the flux and movement of life, the incessant change from infancy to old age which he sees in his own life, as well as in the lives of Neville, Louis, Susan, Jinny, and Rhoda, Bernard employs the cloudscape symbolically.

Lying in a ditch on a stormy day, when it has been raining, then enormous clouds come marching over the sky, tattered clouds, wisps of clouds. What delights me then is the confusion, the height, the indifference and the fury. Great clouds always changing, and movement; something sulphurous and sinister, bowled up, helter-skelter; towering, trailing, broken off, lost, and I forgotten, minute, in a ditch. (p. 169)

Thus like Rabindranath Tagore who, in saying, 'I am like the remnant of an Autumn cloud', uses cloud imagery for an individual, Bernard suggests various individuals of all types and shapes in speaking of 'enormous clouds', 'tattered clouds', and 'wisps of clouds'. He also vividly portrays the change that life undergoes by describing the change and movement of the clouds —trailing, breaking off, and getting lost.

Yet another symbol for change that Virginia Woolf uses in this as well as in some of her other novels is the movement of traffic.

They pass the window of this eating-shop incessantly. Motor-cars, vans, motor-omnibuses; and again motor-omnibuses, vans, motor-cars—they pass the window ..... (They go on passing, they go on passing in disorderly procession.) (pp. 66–67)

This incessant movement of the passing vehicles, the bobbing up and down of hats in disorderly fashion, the perpetual opening and shutting of the door of the eating-shop with its rhythm like a waltz tune, eddying in and out, round and round, effectively conveys the idea of the flux and agitation of life (pp. 66–68). The effect of these symbols is reinforced and heightened by introducing more images that suggest change and movement.

Tuesday follows Monday; then comes Wednesday ..... Opening and shutting, shutting and opening, with increasing hum and sturdiness, the haste and fever of youth are drawn into service until the whole being seems to expand in and out like the mainspring of a clock. How fast the stream flows from January to December! (pp. 182–3)

Tuesday following Monday, the year flowing from January to
December, and the opening and shutting of the mainspring of
the clock, all being apt symbols of time, convey a sensation of
the flux and the agitation of floating life.

More difficult to express than the vitality and flux of life is
the psychological complexity of it. Just as Virginia Woolf in
Mr. Bennett and Mrs. Brown complains that Mr. Bennett while
looking at Mrs. Brown sees only the brooch that she wears or the
mended pair of gloves and not Mrs. Brown herself, Bernard in
the same way, talking to the stranger before whom he is
summing up his life, points out:

You see me, sitting at a table opposite you, a rather heavy, elderly
man, grey at the temples. You see me take my napkin and unfold
it. You see me pour myself out a glass of wine. And you see behind
me the door opening, and people passing. But ..... (p. 169)

But that is not the real Bernard. That is not his life. Bernard is
like an alive, deep rushing stream, as he says,

There is always deep below it, even when we arrive punctually at
the appointed time with our white waistcoats and polite formalities,
a rushing stream of broken dreams, nursery rhymes, street cries,
half-finished sentences and sights—elm trees, willow trees, gardeners
sweeping, women writing—that rise and sink even as we hand a lady
down to dinner. (p. 181)

What Bernard wants the stranger to know, and Virginia Woolf
wants the reader to realize, is that a person is neither merely
that part which is seen socially—a man with a white waistcoat
—nor is he merely his conscious acts—handing the lady down
to dinner—but he has also, as the modern psychologists point
out, a sub- as well as an unconscious mind: a storehouse of all
the sensations experienced during his journey through life, of
all the impressions received from a few intimate friends and
from thousands and thousands of strangers casually met or
hurriedly passed by in the streets, or in the imaginative world of
letters. This storehouse of forgotten or dead memories—the
individual as well as the collective unconscious mind—has in it
things both sublime and ridiculous, poetry as well as nonsense.
Bernard's humming 'Hark, hark, the dogs do bark', 'Come
away, come away death', and 'Let me not to the marriage of
true minds' (p. 184), and his murmuring 'Pillicock sat on

i

Pillicock's hill' or 'The World's great age begins anew' (p. 200), become symbolic of the poetry and nonsense of human life, of Bernard's mysticism, Neville's philosophy, Louis' timidity, Susan's femininity, Rhoda's dreaming, and Jinny's zest for life, of the different things sublime and sordid that constitute life. Thus Bernard conveys to the stranger those ideas that Virginia Woolf has expressed herself in her critical essay on Montaigne. Explaining the variegated nature of human life, she remarks,

This soul, or life within us, by no means agrees with the life outside us ..... Really she is the strangest creature in the world, far from heroic, variable as a weathercock, 'bashful, insolent; chaste, lustful; prating, silent; laborious, delicate; ingenious, heavy; melancholic, pleasant; lying, true; knowing, ignorant; liberal, covetous, and prodigal'—in short, so complex, so indefinite, corresponding so little to the version which does duty for her in public, that a man might spend his life merely in trying to run her to earth.

(*The Common Reader*, First Series, pp. 86–87)

Life *is* indeed, as Bernard tries to express it through another symbol, a symphony. It has 'its concord and its discord, and its tunes on top and its complicated bass beneath' (p. 182). And, like a poem, life cannot be understood without effort. Neville rightly explains this point when he says:

To read this poem one must have myriad eyes, like one of those lamps that turn on slabs of racing water at midnight in the Atlantic, when perhaps only a spray of seaweed pricks the surface, or suddenly the waves gape and up shoulders a monster. One must put aside antipathies and jealousies and not interrupt. One must have patience and infinite care and let the light sound, whether of spiders' delicate feet on a leaf or the chuckle of water in some irrelevant drain-pipe, unfold too. Nothing is to be rejected in fear or horror ..... There are no commas or semi-colons. The lines do not run in convenient lengths. Much is sheer nonsense. One must be sceptical, but throw caution to the winds and when the door opens accept absolutely.

(pp. 141–2)

Virginia Woolf in *The Waves* not only has shown the complexity of human life and personality, but also has explained the way to comprehend it. One must have an unprejudiced mind.

One must not try to make life conform to pre-conceived fixed
laws, because in life, as in Neville's poem, there are no 'commas'
nor have the lines 'convenient lengths', and because, as
Virginia Woolf says in 'Montaigne', 'Movement and change are
the essence of our being; rigidity is death; conformity is death
.....', therefore, the moment 'we begin to protest, to attitudi-
nise, to lay down laws, we perish.'[1] We perish because we cannot
see life in its totality, living pulsating life, not a dead statue
or a truncated, amputated part of it. One must be patient with
life and handle it with care. If one is able to accept it absolutely,
then one is able to understand it, to see its beauty, and be able
to proclaim repeatedly with Bernard that 'Life is pleasant.
Life is good'.[2]

Having explained the flux and agitation that one sees in life,
and having elucidated some of the hidden layers of the mind of
man whose deeps, as Baudelaire says, are fathomless, Bernard
voices his doubts regarding life in its first two aspects. 'Yet some
doubt remains, some note of interrogation,' (p. 190) he says,
because he wants the stranger to realize that the life of the self,
which, with Tuesday following Monday, Wednesday Tuesday,
with their ripples of wellbeing repeating the same curve of
rhythm, 'grows rings' thus making its identity robust (p. 186),
is but a shadow seen in a cave. He wants the stranger to
know that this is not the substance, and that one can only find
real life by dying to self. Then, employing the eclipse of the
sun symbolically, Bernard explains the dying to self and
being reborn into spirit—the life that has in it the essence of
reality.

The woods had vanished; the earth was a waste of shadow. No
sound broke the silence of the wintry landscape. No cock crowed;
no smoke rose; no train moved. A man without a self, I said. A heavy
body leaning on a gate. A dead man. With dispassionate despair,
with entire disillusionment, I surveyed the dust dance; my life,
my friends' lives, and those fabulous presences, men with brooms,
women writing, the willow tree by the river—clouds and phantoms
made of dust too, of dust that changed, as clouds lose and gain and
take gold or red and lose their summits and billow this way and that,
mutable, vain. I, carrying a notebook, making phrases, had recorded

---

[1] *The Common Reader*, First Series, p. 90.
[2] *The Waves*, pp. 182, 185, 186, 192.

mere changes; a shadow, I had been sedulous to take note of
shadows.[1]   (p. 202)

Just as under the eclipse the flourishing full foliage of earth
appears to be withered, brittle and false, similarly the full life
that Bernard had lived appeared to him to be a mere shadow
when he viewed it after having died to self, that is, from a
spiritual point of view. As on the return of the light of the sun
the earth is reborn, rolling in waves of colour, so Bernard, on
being reborn to the life of spirit, feels rejuvenated:

I saw but was not seen. I walked unshadowed; I came unheralded.
From me had dropped the old cloak, the old response; the hollowed
hand that beats back sounds. Thin as a ghost, leaving no trace
where I trod, perceiving merely, I walked alone in a new world,
never trodden; brushing new flowers, unable to speak save in a
child's words of one syllable; without shelter from phrases—I who
have made so many; unattended, I who have always gone with my
kind; solitary, I who have always had someone to share the empty
grate, or the cupboard with its hanging loop of gold.   (p. 203)

In this 'flight of the alone to the Alone', as Plotinus calls it, in
this state of transcendency, of fullness of life, Bernard feels

Immeasurably receptive, holding everything, trembling with fullness, yet clear, contained—so my being seems, now that desire
urges it no more out and away; now that curiosity no longer dyes it
a thousand colours. It lies deep, tideless, immune, now that he is
dead the man I called 'Bernard' ..... But now let the door open, the
glass door that is for ever turning on its hinges. Let a woman come,
let a young man in evening-dress with a moustache sit down: is
there anything that they can tell me? No. I know all that, too .....
So now, taking upon me the mystery of things, I could go like a
spy without leaving this place, without stirring from my chair. I can
visit the remote verges of the desert lands .....   (pp. 206–7)

In these moments of illumination attained by being silent and
alone—'myself being myself' (p. 210)—he is 'tideless' and
'immune' like the still calm sea, he can know a thing without
being told about it, and he is free to go anywhere he likes. Mrs.
Ramsay in *To the Lighthouse*—another mystic—has feelings simi-

---

[1] Virginia Woolf had seen the total eclipse of the sun in June 1927,
when she felt, 'The earth was dead,' and then, 'It was like recovery.' Her
sketch of the eclipse is given in *Diary*, pp. 109–12.

lar to those of Bernard whenever the stroking light of the lighthouse bursts 'some sealed vessel in her brain'.[1] She, too, wants
to be 'herself by herself', and 'To be silent'; to be alone. Like
Bernard, she also feels that 'all the being and the doing, expansive, glittering, vocal' evaporates, and one becomes 'something invisible to others'. It is then that 'her horizon seemed to
her limitless', and that 'there was freedom, there was peace'.[2]

This state of illumination, experienced by both Mrs. Ramsay
and Bernard, which gives them freedom and peace, does not
and cannot last perpetually. It is true what Donne has said
in 'The Broken Heart' about love:

> He is stark mad, whoever says,
>   That he hath been in love an hour,
> Yet not that love so soon decays
>   But that it can ten in less space devour.

The human frame cannot stand the strain of intense and con-
suming passion for long, and even less the intensity of spiritual
communion. Besides, man, being a body as well, is governed by
the needs of the body too. It brings him down to earth. That is
what Bernard means when he says, 'I have walked bang into
the pillar-box ..... Lord, how unutterably disgusting life is!
What dirty tricks it plays us, one moment free; the next, this'
(p. 207). Bernard—'an elderly man who is getting rather heavy
and dislikes exertion' (p. 210)—must take himself off and
catch some last train. He must indulge in bodily actions.

However short-lived these states of illumination may be,
they enlarge one's vision, and make one realize that in reality
one is a spirit that can see but is not seen, that can know everything without being told anything, that is 'unconfined and
capable of being everywhere on the verge of things and here
too' (p. 207), and that 'can change no more' (p. 209). Immune
from change, it is deathless. It only changes its form, it never
dies. Like the breaking wave that, changing its shape, turns into
its original form, the spirit, casting away the body that it wears,
attains its pristine form and glory—the still point of the revolv-
ing wheel. Bernard, having realized this, knows that he might,
like the waves that 'rise and fall and fall and rise again', be
renewed, or might awake to another dawn in pastures new, but

---

[1] *To the Lighthouse*, p. 103.   [2] Ibid., pp. 99–100.

being in essence 'reality' he, like the sea, will never cease to be. With this vision Bernard is able to fling himself unvanquished and unyielding against Death. For him, 'Death is swallowed up; victory is won'. He can say with the Apostle Paul, 'O death, where is your victory? O Death, where is your sting?'[1]

---

[1] *New English Bible*, I Cor. 15, 54–55.

CHAPTER EIGHT

The Years

I<small>N</small> *The Years* Virginia Woolf tries to show society in its every facet—'sex, education, life etc.' Unlike *Mrs. Dalloway* and *The Waves*, it portrays what she calls, the 'ordinary waking Arnold Bennett life'.[1] Like *The Voyage Out* and *Night and Day*, therefore, there is a great deal of externality in it. Concerned less with individuals and more with 'the whole of the present society',[2] Virginia Woolf stresses in it the changes that society undergoes. The Pargiters, like the Forsytes in Galsworthy's *Forsyte Saga*, become symbolic of changing middle-class society.

Virginia Woolf starts the different sections of *The Years* with descriptions of the different seasons, just as she starts the different sections of *The Waves* with descriptions of the different stages of the sun in its diurnal course. Autumn, spring and summer, with rain, wind, and sunshine, and with falling leaves and burning weeds, symbolize the various states of mind of individuals, as well as of society. The changing seasons also suggest the passage of time—of the years.

Virginia Woolf mentions rain with its 'sudden squalls' or a 'steady downpour' at eight different places in the first section. To heighten this effect she also mentions a 'damp earthy smell', 'damp pavements', and 'damp heavy air'. This rain with its accompanying dampness externalizes the lack of warmth of feelings as shown in the callousness of Colonel Pargiter and his 'favourite daughter', Delia, in the bitter hostility between Milly and Delia, in the unsympathetic behaviour of Mrs. Malone, and in the petty bickerings of Kitty and her mother. While Rose Pargiter is lying dead, her husband is having an affair with Mira—'a little fluffy looking' young woman. Both Colonel Pargiter and Delia, who 'were too much alike', as 'each knew

---

[1] *Diary*, pp. 189, 208. (At first V.W. called this novel *The Pargiters*.)
[2] Ibid., p. 191.

what the other was feeling' (p. 38), want Rose Pargiter to die.
Sitting in his club the Colonel sees that people are settling
down in London for the season and he feels that for him there
would be no season, because his wife 'was dying; but she did
not die' (p. 4). Delia thinks that her mother 'soft, decayed but
everlasting', is 'an obstacle, a prevention, an impediment to all
life' (p. 22). She longs for her mother's death. Therefore, 'an
extraordinary feeling of relief and excitement' possesses her
when Crosby informs the Colonel that the Mistress had been
taken worse. 'It has come,' she says to herself, 'it has come'
(p. 38). When Dr. Prentice reports that she is rallying for the
time being, Delia, clenching her hands beneath her mother's
picture cries, 'You're not going to die—never, never!' (p. 40).
Similarly on another occasion when, hearing a bell ring, both
Eleanor and Morris rush to their mother's sick-room, Delia
thinks, 'But what's the good? ..... It's only another false alarm.'
Then glancing at the portrait of her mother, she says bitterly,
'You're not going to die—you're not going to die!' (p. 47).

There is also lack of affection between Delia and Milly.
When Colonel Pargiter told them that old Burke had asked him
to bring one of them to dinner, as Robin was back on leave,

Eleanor, sitting on her low chair, saw a curious look first on Milly's
face, then on Delia's. She had an impression of hostility between
them ..... There was something strained in the atmosphere, Eleanor
felt.   (pp. 14–15)

Martin and Rose, too, are shown quarrelling frequently. This
trait Eleanor remembers throughout her life: 'They always
bickered, Eleanor thought—Martin and Rose' (p. 168)
They themselves talk about it at Delia's party.

'She always was a spitfire,' said Martin, turning to Peggy.
'And they always put the blame on me,' Rose said. '*He* had the
school-room. Where was I to sit? "Oh, run away and play in the
nursery!" ' She waved her hand.
'And so she went into the bathroom and cut her wrist with a
knife,' Martin jeered.   (p. 387)

It is raining in Oxford, too, and there we are shown Mrs.
Malone's lack of affection for her cousin, Rose Pargiter, and
the petty bickering between her and her daughter, Kitty.

When Mrs. Malone hears about the death of her cousin, she asks for her engagement book and puts off the dinner that was to be held on Monday. When Kitty suggests that she should also cancel 'the Lotham's party on Wednesday', Mrs. Malone replies sharply, 'we can't put off everything' (p. 85). This reply clearly reflects both her feelings for her cousin, and her relationship with Kitty. When Mrs. Malone tauntingly points out that Kitty should help her father if it bores her helping her mother, Kitty admits guiltily,

'I haven't been to Papa lately. But then there's always something .....'
   'Naturally,' said Mrs. Malone, 'with a man in your father's position .....' Kitty sat silent. They both sat silent. They both disliked this petty bickering; they both detested these recurring scenes; and yet they seemed inevitable.   (p. 86)

Virginia Woolf also uses a tea-kettle and a flickering flame to symbolize the lack of family affections.

'It's not boiling,' said Milly Pargiter, looking at the tea-kettle .....
'Not nearly boiling,' she repeated ..... A feeble little flame flickered up and down beneath the brass bowl .....
   Milly took a hairpin from her head and began to fray the wick into separate strands so as to increase the size of the flame ..... A gnat's voice began to wail under the kettle.   (pp. 8–9)

In contrast to the kettles that are always boiling in *Night and Day* both at the Hilberys' and at the Denhams', where there is sociability and family affection, the fact that in *The Years* the kettle will not boil, becomes, as Bernard Blackstone points out, a symbol of the lack of these feelings.[1]
   Mira, like Florinda and Fanny in *Jacob's Room*, represents the obscene and the lewd side of life. The 'smell in the house', the 'dirty clothes hanging on a line', and the room littered with 'too many little objects', along with Mira's 'untidy' hair, suggesting dirt and disorder, become symbols of her unclean life. Behind the figure of Mira, whom we meet in the 1880 and the 1891 sections of *The Years*, we also have a glimpse of the

[1] Blackstone, op. cit., p. 195.

prostitutes of London. Mira thus shows up the levity of the Victorian age.[1]

The stains and smudges, and the greasy and smeared things that Virginia Woolf mentions at many places in *The Years*, like the red patch behind the ear of Mira's dog, suggest uncleanliness. There is 'a green smudge' on Rose's pinafore (p. 9), and a 'dark stain' on the large armchair where Colonel Pargiter used to rest his head (p. 17). The college buildings in Oxford are 'red-stained' and 'yellow-stained' (p. 53), and the pavements are 'greasy' (p. 49). The window, where the Jew boy sat mugging up Greek, is also 'smeared' (p. 66).

In the next section falling leaves and smoke are used symbolically to suggest the mental states of the characters mentioned in it. When Colonel Pargiter, while talking to Eleanor, looked out at the back garden,

'How the leaves are falling!' he remarked.
'Yes,' she said. 'They're burning weeds.'
He stood looking at the smoke for a moment.
'Burning weeds,' he repeated, and stopped.   (p. 98)

When he goes to Browne Street and takes a birthday present for Magdalena, smoke blows 'straight at him' and makes his eyes water (pp. 126–7). The smoke that blows straight at his face and fills up the room symbolizes the state of his mind at that particular period of his life when 'he was getting rather too red and heavy' (p. 98), and also 'slower and slower' (p. 97). It indicates a mind that, becoming old, decrepit, and foggy, had lost its quickness and clarity. When he wanted to talk to Eugénie about his entanglement with Mira, he could not make up his mind to do so. 'He wanted to tell her about Mira. But he told her about the family' (pp. 131–2). On leaving the house as he thought about the children, he paused on the doorstep and looked out into the street.

It was quite dark; lamps were lit; the autumn was drawing in; and

---

[1] R. C. K. Ensor in *Oxford History of England*, Vol. XIV, 1960, p. 170, while defending the Victorians against a charge of sexual levity, indirectly admits it when he says,
'Probably at the bottom of society there was a greater amount of coarse prostitution than now ..... But it is very significant that when well-to-do Victorians gave way to vice they commonly went to Paris to indulge it.'

as he marched up the dark windy street, now spotted with raindrops, a puff of smoke blew full in his face; and leaves were falling.

(p. 136)

The dark street with blowing smoke, and autumn with its falling leaves, become apt symbols of Colonel Pargiter's age. The smoky darkness not only indicates the indistinct old age that lay before him, but also suggests the foggy state of his mind. Similarly the falling leaves suggest the withering and falling off of his mental and physical qualities, and his being bereft of his children who were leaving him as they grew up.

The autumn wind twitching the leaves off the trees, the smoke drifting over the flaming dahlias or hanging in veils over the spires and domes, and the mist in the wood or hanging thick in the East End by the river (pp. 94–96), besides symbolizing the mental state of Abel Pargiter, give us an insight into Eleanor's state of mind. Having passed the prime of her life, she had become,

a well-known type; with a bag; philanthropic; well nourished; a spinster; a virgin; like all the women of her class, cold.   (p. 108)

The dead leaves, which damage the new building by choking the gutter, are an appropriate symbol of Eleanor's emotions and instincts which, being denied natural outlet into married life and motherhood, have atrophied and turned her into a cold spinster. This effect Virginia Woolf also heightens by using 'the sunflower on the terra-cotta plaque' as a symbol.

She gave one look at the sunflower on the terra-cotta plaque. That symbol of her girlish sentiment amused her grimly. She had meant it to signify flowers, fields in the heart of London; but now it was cracked.   (p. 107)

The cracked flower becomes a symbol of the life that had not bloomed into a happy married one.

Virginia Woolf uses the falling leaves of autumn also to suggest death. When Eleanor was walking through London, she

looked at a placard that was crumpled across a boy's legs. 'Death' was written in very large black letters.

Then the placard blew straight, and she read another word: 'Parnell.'

'Dead' ..... she repeated. 'Parnell' ..... The traffic hummed far off; she could just hear the paper-boys crying death ..... death ..... death. The leaves were falling ..... Then she went to the Square and climbed the stairs and rattled at the door again. But there was no sound within. She stood for a moment watching the leaves fall; she heard the paper-boys crying ..... Then a leaf fell.   (pp. 120–3)

In these pages Virginia Woolf describes in a masterly way the seeping of an incident into a person's consciousness. How, starting from the subconscious, it works through into the conscious mind, and then yields its full significance. 'Then a leaf fell' becomes a forceful symbol of Parnell's death.

Virginia Woolf suggests the outer show and the inner hollowness of well-to-do middle-class society by juxtaposing the well-furnished big houses and the slums of London, the filigree spires of churches and the pipes and drains beneath them, and the outer majestic garments and the inner shallow tastes of Mr. Justice Curry.

Suddenly a door was thrown open. The usher demanded silence for his lordship. There was silence; everybody stood up; and the Judge came in ..... Eleanor felt a little thrill of awe run through her. That was old Curry. But how transformed! Last time she had seen him he was sitting at the head of a dinner-table ..... and he had taken her, with a candle, round the drawing-room to look at his old oak. But now, there he was, awful, magisterial, in his robes .....

She fidgeted. The air was fuggy; the light dim; and the Judge now that the first glamour had worn off, looked fretful; no longer immune from human weakness, and she remembered with a smile how gullible he was, there in that hideous house in Queen's Gate, about old oak. 'This I picked up at Whitby,' he had said. And it was a sham.   (pp. 116–19)

The awful, magisterial appearance of the Judge who is supposed to be able to arrive at sound and correct notions about things contrasted with his inability to discriminate between genuine and sham old oak, even though he is passionately interested in it, besides forming a delightful caricature of an ineffective judge, signifies the inner shallowness of a pompous society.

Like the rain and dampness, and the smoke and falling leaves of the previous sections, music and dance provide a symbolic background to the third section of *The Years*.

It was midsummer; and the nights were hot .....

All the windows were open. Music sounded. From behind crimson curtains, rendered semi-transparent and sometimes blowing wide came the sound of the eternal waltz—After the ball is over, after the dance is done—like a serpent that swallowed its own tail, since the ring was complete from Hammersmith to Shoreditch. Over and over again it was repeated by trombones outside public houses; errand boys whistled it; bands inside private rooms where people were dancing played it.   (pp. 138-9)

This midsummer heat with its music and dancing not only symbolizes the lively and bubbling youth of Maggie and Martin, but also represents 'the prime of life with all one's faculties about one' which Digby and Eugénie had reached— Eugénie especially, who 'came across the room, beaming, glowing' (p. 150) and moved with extraordinary stateliness, whose body seemed to be music personified. The music is short lived in this section, so is the second Pargiter family—Sir Digby and Lady Pargiter and hence the prosperity of Maggie and Sara, their daughters.

But the wind that blows in the next section of the book is a more powerful symbol.

It was March and the wind was blowing. But it was not 'blowing'. It was scraping, scourging. It was so cruel. So unbecoming. Not merely did it bleach faces and raise red spots on noses; it tweaked up skirts; showed stout legs; made trousers reveal skeleton shins. There was no roundness, no fruit in it. Rather it was like the curve of a scythe which cuts, not corn usefully; but destroys, revelling in sheer sterility ..... It tossed up rotten leaves, gave them another span of degraded existence; scorned, derided them, yet had nothing to put in the place of the scorned, the derided ..... Uncreative, un-productive, yelling its joy in destruction.   (p. 157)

This description of the blowing wind, like the descriptions of the sun, the sea, and the birds in *The Waves*, symbolically represents what is about to happen in the succeeding section. The cutting and destroying wind represents the death of Eugénie and Digby, who die in the prime of their lives. Its tossing up of the rotten leaves and giving them another span of degraded existence signifies the condition of old Colonel Pargiter who had grown 'inert and ponderous after his stroke'. The scraping wind also suggests the shearing off of Eleanor's mental faculties: she 'felt old, heavy and dull', and could not any longer remember how 'Rose had locked herself in the bathroom with a knife and cut her wrist' (p. 170); nor could she recall that there was a flower in the grass in their mother's picture (p. 171).

When Rose went to luncheon with Maggie and Sara they started talking about Abercorn Terrace.

> Her past seemed to be rising above her present. And for some reason she wanted to talk about her past; to tell them something about herself that she had never told anybody—something hidden. She paused, gazing at the flowers in the middle of the table without seeing them. There was a blue knot in the yellow glaze she noted ..... It puzzled her; it made her feel that she was two different people at the same time; that she was living at two different times at the same moment. She was a little girl wearing a pink frock; and here she was in this room, now .....
>
> What is the use, she thought, of trying to tell people about one's past? What is one's past? She stared at the pot with the blue knot loosely tied in the yellow glaze.   (pp.179–80)

Rose, like Eleanor who 'seemed to divide herself into two' (p. 189), and like Kitty and the youth who were in two worlds at once (pp. 196–200), feels that there is, like an outer clock time and inner *durée*, an outer person and an inner personality —a bunch of one's past memories. 'The blue knot loosely tied' that Rose sees becomes an apt symbol of those memories and the different layers of personality which, Virginia Woolf feels, cannot be conveyed adequately to others.

Describing the pre-war division of classes in 'The Leaning Tower' Virginia Woolf says,

> ..... I see that life divided up, herded together, into many different classes. There is the aristocracy; the landed gentry; the professional class; the commercial class; the working class; and there, in one dark blot, is the great class which is called simply and comprehensively 'The Poor'.   (*The Moment and Other Essays*, pp. 108–9)

The brawling people whom Sara sees outside the public house, and the drunken Upcher and his abusive wife whose quarrel Maggie and Sara hear—'nasty little creatures, driven by uncontrollable lusts' (p. 203), roaring and cursing and creating violence and unrest become, like the inhabitants of Whitechapel graphically described by Virginia Woolf in *Flush*, an image of that 'great class' which, according to Charles Booth's estimate constituted 30·7 per cent. of the inhabitants of London in 1888.[1] When there was a sound of brawling in the street outside, Sara went to the window and saw that a crowd had gathered outside the public house where a man was being thrown out. After some time Sara and Maggie heard that

somebody was hammering on the door of the next house. The hammering stopped. Then it began again—hammer, hammer, hammer.

They listened.

'Upcher's come home drunk and wants to be let in,' said Maggie .....

..... A window was thrown open. A woman's voice was heard shrieking abuse at the man. He bawled back in a thick drunken voice from the doorstep. Then the door slammed.

They listened.

'Now he'll stagger against the wall and be sick,' said Maggie.

(pp. 204–5)

Like the stains on buildings, the smudges on clothes, and the illness and deformity of various characters that we come across in *The Years*, these brawling, staggering, and vomiting men are an evocative image of the sickness and deformity of society before the First World War.

Kitty's party, where the ladies indulged in 'a battledore and shuttlecock talk' which though animated 'lacked substance' (p. 279), and where, in spite of the fine clothes and looks that were complimented upon after dinner, people's 'faces looked harassed, worried; their hands moved restlessly' (p. 280), portrays their trivial enjoyments and sham refinements. On hearing Lady Margaret tell a 'rather coarse' story, Kitty felt like fleecing them 'of their clothes, of their jewels, of their intrigues, of their gossip' to show up their useless and worthless life which was like an empty shuttle weaving the wind. Later on, Lady Warburton, who went downstairs like a crab, was robing herself:

Now she was accepting her cloak with a violet slash in it; now her furs. A bag dangled from her wrist. She was hung about with

Life and Labour of the People in London, Vol. I, 1902, p. 21.

chains; her fingers were knobbed with rings. Her sharp stone-coloured face, riddled with lines and wrinkled with creases, looked out from its soft nest of fur and laces .....

The nineteenth century going to bed, Martin said to himself as he watched her hobble down the steps on the arm of her footman.

(p. 287)

Lady Warburton with her slashed cloak, jewels, furs and laces, like the plumed generals, the wigged judges, and the ermined professors of *Three Guineas*, becomes symbolic of possessions and the arrogant display of them, which, Virginia Woolf thinks, lead to greed and competition—two major causes of international wars.

When the party is over Kitty slips the rings from her fingers, kicks off the tight 'satin shoe'—symbol, as in *Jacob's Room*, of emasculated civilization,[1] in contrast to Jacob's and Martin's pairs of old shoes—she puts off her party dress and changes into a travelling dress with a tweed travelling hat, thus looking 'quite a different person; the person she liked being' (p. 288). Then she travels off to the North of England. All these actions, like Jacob's leaving London for Greece, are symbolic of her rejection of the unnatural life of London with its sham refinement, its coarseness of drunken, brawling men and tipsy, swaying girls.

So when Londoners were still asleep, Kitty was sauntering out in the fields on 'a perfect May morning' with the dew shining 'red, violet, gold on the trembling tips of the grass blades'. In contrast to London with its fret and fury, the countryside becomes symbolic of peace and happiness. It is there that Kitty, 'was happy, completely'. Nature with her shining dew, 'pale spring flowers, the loveliest of the year ..... trembling on cushions of green moss', the singing wind and murmuring land—'uncultivated, uninhabited, existing by itself, for itself' (pp. 299–300)—becomes an external image of Kitty's state of mind. Kitty feels happy and exhilarated as did John Ruskin who felt

a continual perception of sanctity in the whole of nature, from the slightest thing to the vastest, an instinctive awe, mixed with delight, an indefinable thrill, such as we sometimes imagine to indicate the presence of a disembodied spirit.[2]

[1] See p. 51 above.   [2] *Modern Painters*, Vol. III, 1904, p. 367.

In this section Kitty, besides being happy, 'was in the prime of life; she was vigorous' (p. 300). Martin, too, was young: 'I'm young, he thought, I'm in the prime of life.' Maggie also was happily married. To evoke these feelings of young, happy life, Virginia Woolf employs symbolic background. This section opens with the following description:

It was a brilliant spring; the day was radiant. Even the air seemed to have a burr in it as it touched the tree tops; it vibrated, it rippled.
(p. 241)

Besides these opening sentences and the passages describing Kitty's sauntering in the woods, we come across throughout this section expressions such as the 'tang of earth', the 'faint smell of spring' (p. 255), 'fresh and full of sweetness' (p. 257), and 'full of the stir, the potency, the fecundity of spring' (p. 264).

In the section '1917' after the raid was over Sara proposed and they all drank 'To the New World'. Eleanor sat musing and wanted to know how the world was going to improve. Nicholas explained that it was only a question of learning about the soul, of living more naturally.

'The soul—the whole being,' he explained. He hollowed his hands as if to enclose a circle. 'It wishes to expand; to adventure; to form—new combinations?'

'Yes, yes,' she said, as if to assure him that his words were right.

'Whereas now,'—he drew himself together; put his feet together; he looked like an old lady who is afraid of mice—'this is how we live, screwed up into one hard little, tight little—knot?'

'Knot, knot—yes, that's right,' she nodded.

'Each in his own little cubicle; each with his own cross or holy book; each with his fire, his wife .....'
(p. 319)

Nicholas, in company with Rabindranath Tagore, Romain Rolland and Wilfred Owen, has the courage to decry petty nationalism. Rabindranath Tagore in *Nationalism* feels that the idea of the nation is a 'powerful anaesthetic' under whose influence people pursue self-seeking; Romain Rolland in *Above the Battle* decries 'idols of religion and nationality'; and Wilfred Owen deplores 'the dogma of national church' and 'pure patriotism'. Surmounting these barriers they want our souls to expand and form new combinations. Virginia Woolf herself expounds these ideas in *Three Guineas*. There she talks about learning the art of understanding other people's lives and minds, about exploring ways and means in which 'mind and body can be made to co-operate; discover new combinations make good wholes in human life', and about ridding oneself 'of pride of nationality in the first place; also of religious pride, college pride .....' Thus Nicholas does not want people and nations to shrivel up into hard tight knots, and symbolically he draws himself together like an old lady afraid of mice.

Light is an archetypal symbol for knowledge and spiritual illumination. Virginia Woolf, therefore, anticipating the realization that Eleanor is to arrive at and the illumination that she is going to have in the final section of *The Years*, starts that section with a description of a scene aglow with light, and she ends it with the ever increasing light of the rising dawn.

It was a summer evening; the sun was setting; the sky was blue still, but tinged with gold, as if a thin veil of gauze hung over it, and here and there in the gold-blue amplitude an island of cloud lay suspended ..... An edge of light surrounded everything. A red-gold fume rose from dust on the roads. Even the little red brick villas on the high roads had become porous, incandescent with light, and the flowers in cottage gardens, lilac and pink like cotton dresses, shone veined as if lit from within. Faces of people standing at cottage doors or padding along pavements showed the same red glow as they fronted the slowly sinking sun.   (p. 329)

The sky tinged with gold, the incandescent villas, the rising red-gold fumes, and the flowers lit up from within become symbolic of the state of Eleanor's mind. They also symbolize the realization of the meaning of life and personality that the other two meditative Pargiters—Peggy and North—arrive at. While driving to attend Delia's party, Peggy

was alone with Eleanor in the cab. And they were passing houses. Where does she begin, and where do I end? she thought ..... On they drove. They were two living people, driving across London; two sparks of life enclosed in two separate bodies; and those sparks of life enclosed in two separate bodies are at this moment, she thought, driving past a picture palace. But what is this moment; and what are we?   (p. 360)

Peggy is deeply interested in knowing what exactly we are. She muses again about 'What makes up a person' (p. 380)—

body, or body-mind, or something else. Being a doctor she had realized that 'Doctors know very little about the body; absolutely nothing about the mind' (p. 415). A materialistic conception of man does not satisfy her, and she is displeased with the type of life that other people are visualizing for North: 'How he's to live, where he's to live.' Fearing that North will follow the life of a materialist, she addresses him thus:

'You'll marry. You'll have children. What'll you do then? Make money. Write little books to make money ..... You'll write one little book, and then another little book ..... instead of living ..... living differently, differently'.   (p. 421)

She wanted him to live differently, to acquire a 'state of being' which she can see but cannot express properly, 'in which there was real laughter, real happiness, and this fractured world was whole; whole, and free' (p. 420). North can sense it, too, but cannot express it. Mustering up courage to speak the truth,

'What you said was true,' he blurted out, '..... quite true.' It was what she meant that was true, he corrected himself; her feeling, not her words. He felt her feeling now; it was not about him; it was about other people; about another world, a new world .....
But Peggy was waiting, she was watching him .....
'..... To live differently ..... differently,' he repeated. Those were her words; they did not altogether fit his meaning; but he had to use them.   (p. 456)

Like Peggy, who thought that living differently is not living at a different place but living in a different kind of way, North, too, realizes that it is not a matter of, as Renny had mistaken it to be, 'the other world' (p. 418), nor was it a simplified world which was 'one jelly, one mass ..... a rice pudding world' (p. 442), but it was the state of being 'a new ripple in human consciousness', 'the bubble and the stream, the stream and the bubble—myself and the world together' (p. 443). This can be achieved, he felt, by reforming ourselves (p. 437), and by trying to know 'what's solid, what's true' in our own and in other people's lives (p. 443).
Eleanor, too, becomes conscious of extra-physical life.

There must be another life, she thought, sinking back into her chair, exasperated. Not in dreams; but here and now, in this room, with

living people. She felt as if she were standing on the edge of a
precipice with her hair blown back; she was about to grasp something that just evaded her. There must be another life, here and now,
she repeated. This is too short, too broken. We know nothing, even
about ourselves. We're only just beginning, she thought, to understand, here and there.   (p. 461)

This new ripple of consciousness experienced by Eleanor,
Peggy, and North and making them happy, is perhaps the
answer to the question Eleanor is recorded as asking earlier in
the book—the question she had always wanted to ask about
Christianity: 'God is love, The Kingdom of Heaven is within us,
sayings like that ..... what did they mean?' (p. 166) So the
incandescence of the scene that Virginia Woolf describes at the
beginning of this section externalizes the inner light that these
people see.

    In this section, Abercorn Terrace with its 'one bathroom
and basement' stands for the 'abominable system' of people
living 'boxed up together, telling lies' (p. 239). Eleanor's
moving from there to a 'flat with a shower-bath' (p. 331) not
only represents the technological advancement of the age but
also signifies a change in the mode of life and thought of the
people who became free to live their lives unencumbered by
their large families. This freedom coupled with the new ripple
of consciousness represents the emergence of the new world.
Virginia Woolf's conception of the new world is not like that of
Aldous Huxley's cynical *Brave New World*. It is more like the
brave new world that Miranda senses in *The Tempest*, a world
not of revenge but of forgiveness, not of war but of reconciliation, not of stress and strife but of peace and happiness.

    The Gibbses—Hugh and Milly—'gross, obese, shapeless'
(p. 409), Milly's ring sunk in her finger seeming to North
'flesh grown over diamonds' (p. 402), become, like Lady Warburton, symbols of 'poisoned vanities and parades that breed
competition and jealousy'. They represent the leisured class—
the 'men shot, and the women ..... broke off into innumerable
babies' (p. 404). They, along with the group of the old brothers
and sisters gathered against the window, are the 'old fogies'
who are unable to understand the younger generation represented by the children of the caretaker. When Martin beckons
to the children to speak, 'they gaze solemnly and remain

silent'. The younger generation do not mean to speak, says Peggy. This signifies that the younger generation are not like the leisured middle class who have ample time and money to go to useless parties, to parade their possessions, and to talk and gossip endlessly. The younger generation are working people. They act more and talk less. In the end when those children sing, they sound 'so shrill, so discordant, and so meaningless' to the Pargiters (p. 464). Their sounding shrill and meaningless suggests that the old middle class is unable to comprehend the philosophy of the rising working class. 'But what the devil were they singing?' says Hugh Gibbs. He could not understand a word of it. Out of all the older generation of Pargiters it is Eleanor alone to whom they looked 'so dignified', and for whom their singing was 'beautiful'.

With the rise of the new class, 'It's time to go' for the others. They have to make room for the working class to take its proper place. The room where Delia's party was being held was an estate agent's office. As the party was coming to an end 'the tables were becoming office tables; their legs were the legs of office tables' (p. 465). This setting, too, is symbolic. By going out the Pargiters—symbol of a leisured society—make room for the office people to come in and work. Though to express her idea Virginia Woolf has made use of office imagery, it is significant to note here that the working class which she was visualizing is the working class from which, as she says in *Three Guineas*, Christ 'sprang himself' and from which 'he chose his disciples'.[1]

'The dawn—the new day' (p. 466), like the dawn in *The Waves*, signifies the rising of a new order of society, the ushering in of a new era. While the Pargiters are leaving, Eleanor watches a taxi gliding slowly round the square. It stops in front of a house. A young man gets out, then a girl in a tweed travelling suit follows him. 'There', Eleanor murmurs, as he opens the door and they stand for a moment on the threshold. 'There', she repeats as the door shuts with a thud behind them. Then she turns round into the room and says, 'And now'. The young man and the girl, like Trofimov and Varya in *The Cherry Orchard*, symbolize the younger generation, and suggest youth, strength and hope. 'There' stands for their

[1] Op. cit., London, 1938, p. 221.

stepping on to the scene, 'And now' signifies that it is time for the fogies—the Pargiters—to step off. The setting sun with which the Pargiters' party started is symbolic of their having run their course. The rising sun that brings in the young couple stands for the birth of a new class, of a new vigorous civilization. Far from giving, 'a curious feeling of hopelessness'[1] this novel ends with uplift and renewal.

[1] Deborah Newton: *Virginia Woolf*, Melbourne University Press, 1946, p. 56.

CHAPTER NINE

Between the Acts

VIRGINIA WOOLF started writing *Between the Acts* about April, 1938, and finished its first draft, according to her statement in her diary, on 23 November 1940, when she wrote:

Having this moment finished the Pageant—or Poyntz Hall?—(begun perhaps April 1938) my thoughts turn well up, to write the first chapter of the next book.

On completing its first revision on 26 February 1941, she again recorded the fact as follows:

Finished Pointz Hall, the Pageant, the play—finally *Between the Acts* this morning.

It is clear, therefore, that this novel was written during the threat of war, its outbreak, and the bombardment of London, which wrecked Virginia Woolf's house in Mecklenburgh Square, and completely destroyed her other one in Tavistock Square. While on page after page in her diary she has recorded her reactions to these harrying times, when Leonard Woolf kept enough 'petrol in the garage for suicide should Hitler win',[1] it is remarkable that this novel does not reflect them. We do not find in it any sense of fear, uncertainty and insecurity as we do in *Jacob's Room*. Rather, it shows tranquil recollection and sober judgement—signs of an integrated personality, of a mature and serene artist.

Whereas in *Orlando* and *The Years* Virginia Woolf treats time in its historical perspective showing the changes that a society undergoes, and in *Mrs. Dalloway*, and to a lesser extent in *The Waves*, she shows the inner durée and the outer clock time affecting individual personalities, in *Between the Acts*, bringing all her ideas about time together, she not only records inner, clock, and historical time, but also brings in prehistoric

[1] *Diary*, p. 332.

time. Besides time and its effects, in this novel she gives us a more mature vision of life and reality. The stress here is neither on personal relationships, as seen in *The Voyage Out* and *Night and Day* and *To the Lighthouse*, nor on personality, as shown in *Jacob's Room*, *Mrs. Dalloway* and *The Waves*, nor on society, as portrayed in *Orlando* and *The Years*. The stress is on all aspects of life equally—the physical as well as the spiritual—the social as well as the individual—the active as well as the contemplative.

Because she is portraying this panoramic view of life and, unlike Tolstoy and James Joyce in *War and Peace* and *Ulysses*, is condensing it to its very quintessence, she has to use for this novel a different form and a new technique which includes both extremes of poetic intensity and discursive prose, to express the full gamut of her emotions, and to evoke her vision of variegated life which, to quote from her diary, is composed of 'all life, all art, all waifs and strays—a rambling capricious but somehow unified whole'.[1] Therefore she uses many new symbols and more similes than ever before.

The development of Virginia Woolf's mind is evidenced by her treatment of the character of Lucy Swithin in *Between the Acts*. She is the most inconsequential and yet the most important character in the novel. Like Mrs. Ramsay in *To the Lighthouse*, Eleanor in *The Years*, and even Mrs. Hilbery in *Night and Day* —the contemplatives in her novels—Mrs. Swithin is the least intellectual of all the characters in *Between the Acts*, yet, like her counterparts in the other novels, it is she who gives us an insight into Virginia Woolf's vision of life. Mrs. Swithin is the first major character in her novels to carry 'a cross gleaming gold on her breast' (p. 15). Though her brother Bartholomew makes fun of her cross and her faith, Virginia Woolf, who had written earlier against religion and Christianity in *The Voyage Out* and *Mrs. Dalloway*, does not seem to do so. Turning the pages of the paper, when her brother read out, 'Variable winds; fair average temperature; rain at times', Mrs. Swithin said:

'It's very unsettled. It'll rain, I'm afraid. We can only pray', she added, and fingered her crucifix.

[1] *Diary*, p. 289.

'And provide umbrellas,' said her brother.

Lucy flushed. He had struck her faith. When she said 'pray', he added 'umbrellas'. She half covered the cross with her fingers.

(pp. 30–31)

Again when wanting to know the origin of 'Touch wood', she inquired:

'What's the origin—the origin—of that?'

'Superstition,' he said.

She flushed, and the little breath too was audible that she drew in as once more he struck a blow at her faith. But, brother and sister, flesh and blood was not a barrier, but a mist. Nothing changed their affection; no argument; no fact; no truth. What she saw he didn't; what he saw she didn't—and so on, *ad infinitum*.   (p. 33)

Even though his viewpoint differs, Bartholomew is not either intolerant or indignant like Rachel in *The Voyage Out*, and Clarissa in *Mrs. Dalloway*. On seeing the hospital nurse pray in the hotel chapel, Rachel had come

to the conclusion that the hospital nurse was only slavishly acquiescent, and that the look of satisfaction was produced by no splendid conception of God within her. How, indeed, could she conceive anything far outside her own experience, a woman with a commonplace face like hers, a little round red face, upon which trivial duties and trivial spites had drawn lines, whose weak blue eyes saw without intensity or individuality, whose features were blurred, insensitive, and callous? She was adoring something shallow and smug, clinging to it, so that the obstinate mouth witnessed, with the assiduity of a limpet; nothing would tear her from her demure belief in her own virtue and the virtues of her religion ..... The face of this single worshipper became printed on Rachel's mind with an impression of keen horror, and she had it suddenly revealed to her what Helen meant and St. John meant when they proclaimed their hatred of Christianity. With the violence that now marked her feelings, she rejected all that she had implicitly believed.   (pp. 278–9)

Like the raw girl that she was, Rachel, because of a fallacious argument, came to a wrong conclusion: because one of the worshippers had a commonplace face, therefore she could not have a splendid conception of God; and because the nurse could not have a splendid conception of God, Rachel must hate Christianity and reject belief. Clarissa Dalloway, too, mistaking love and religion for possessiveness and exploitation, had

thought, 'How detestable, how detestable they are!'[1] Bartholomew, on the other hand, does not experience 'sudden
impulse' and 'violent anguish' like Clarissa Dalloway, or
violence of feeling like Rachel. His affection for his sister does
not get ruffled. He not only is tolerant, but also tries to understand her point of view. He asks himself

> why, in Lucy's skull, shaped so much like his own, there existed a
> prayable being? She didn't, he supposed, invest it with hair, teeth
> or toe-nails. It was, he supposed, more of a force or a radiance
> controlling the thrush and the worm; the tulip and the hound; and
> himself, too, an old man with swollen veins. It got her out of her
> bed on a cold morning and sent her down the muddy path to wor-
> ship it .....   (pp. 32–33)

This change of stress from condemnation to toleration and an
attempt to understand faith and religion is the result, it
appears, of Virginia Woolf's renewed interest in religion and
mysticism. During the period between the writing of *Mrs.
Dalloway* and *Between the Acts* she had been reading not only
the religious writers but also the historians and interpreters of
Christianity. On 1 January 1935, when she was engaged upon
writing *The Years*, she writes in her diary:

> ..... and read St. Paul and the papers. I must buy the Old Testament.
> I am reading the Acts of the Apostles. At last I am illuminating that
> dark spot in my reading. What happened in Rome? And there are
> seven volumes of Renan.

So, when Martin goes to see Eleanor, he finds she had been
reading Renan because she

> had always wanted to know about Christianity—how it began;
> what it meant, originally. God is love, The Kingdom of Heaven
> is within us, sayings like that she thought, turning over the pages,
> what did they mean?   (*The Years*, p. 166)

Virginia Woolf herself, like Eleanor in *The Years*, had been
reading Renan and thinking about Christianity. Her interest in
Christianity persisted. In *Three Guineas* which followed *The
Years* and at which she was still working when she had started
writing *Between the Acts*, she quotes St. Paul and Christ. During
this period she also read Pascal as we find from her diary:

---

[1] *Mrs. Dalloway*, p. 139.

..... try to concentrate on Pascal. I can't. Still it's the only way of tuning up, and I get a calm, if not understanding. These pin points of theology need a grasp beyond me.[1]

Taking into consideration these facts, one is tempted to conjecture that Virginia Woolf, who definitely was of a mystical bent of mind, as is clear from *To the Lighthouse* and *The Waves*, had started feeling the need of some type of religious faith. This might be the result of the 'spiritual conversion' which she has mentioned but not explained in her diary.[2] This conversion brings her back to the viewpoint which she held at an earlier age, and about which she wrote in her diary:

I was then writing a long picturesque essay upon the Christian religion, I think; called Religio Laici, I believe, proving that man has need of a God.[3]

Mrs. Swithin, with her belief in God, represents the simple religious faith which, Virginia Woolf seems to feel, the world needs today. The staging of the pageant in aid of the village church in *Between the Acts* attains symbolic value too. It stresses the need for renovating one's faith at a time when 'the motor bike, the motor bus, and the movies', as Mr. Streatfield, the clergyman, thought, were to blame for the absentees from church (p. 93).

God is love, so Mrs. Swithin, a firm believer in Him, is the most tender-hearted of all the characters in this novel, and even of all the mystics in the other novels. Her love for the children is warmer even than their mother's. On seeing the perambulator pass across the lawn, her exclaiming, 'Oh there they are—the darlings!' (p. 31) is an act of simple delight and complete absorption, as compared to Isa Oliver's feelings, tinged as they are with the extraneous idea that the children are a link between herself and Giles—the father of her children (p. 19). It is Mrs. Swithin again who shows concern for their wellbeing by inquiring whether the boy had eaten his breakfast, and whether the baby had any signs of measles (p. 32). In the evening it is Mrs. Swithin again who, thinking about the children, says to Isa, 'I looked in and saw the babies, sound asleep, under the paper roses' (p. 254). Being tender-hearted she, unlike her brother, is considerate of the feelings of others.

[1] *Diary*, p. 314.   [2] Ibid., p. 292.   [3] Ibid., p. 151.

Remembering what her mother had told her about not playing on people's names, she refrains from saying, 'The sandwiches, Sands', because 'Sand and sandwiches clashed' (p. 43). She thinks not only of providing sandwiches and lemonade for the people working in the Barn, but also of feeding the fish in the lily pond.

> The fish had come to the surface. She had nothing to give them— not a crumb of bread. 'Wait, my darlings,' she addressed them. She would trot into the house and ask Mrs. Sands for a biscuit.
>
> (p. 240)

Thus loving both men and fish, she represents the devout person about whom Coleridge says,

> He prayeth well, who loveth well
> Both man and bird and beast.

Because hers is not a momentary vision like matches struck in darkness, nor mere intellectual knowledge, but a living and abiding faith, which is suggested by her act of shielding her cross unconsciously when she felt that her brother had struck her faith (p. 31), her piety affects others. When Mrs. Swithin showed William Dodge over the house, and he saw her lambent eyes,

> he wished to kneel before her, to kiss her hand, and to say: 'At school they held me under a bucket of dirty water, Mrs. Swithin; when I looked up the world was dirty, Mrs. Swithin; so I married; but my child's not my child, Mrs. Swithin. I'm a half-man, Mrs. Swithin; a flickering, mind-divided little snake in the grass, Mrs. Swithin; as Giles saw; but you've healed me .....   (p. 90)

He feels cleansed and healed as would a sick man before the grotto of the Virgin Mary at Lourdes. He feels purified. He becomes able to see the beauty of the visible world.

> 'I'd no notion we looked so nice,' Mrs. Swithin whispered to William. Hadn't she? The children; the pilgrims; behind the pilgrims the trees, and behind them the fields—the beauty of the visible world took his breath away .....
>
> 'Isn't that enough?' William asked himself. Beauty—Isn't that enough?   (p. 100)

Even Mrs. Manresa, the wild child of nature, could not tell a doubtful anecdote in front of Mrs. Swithin.

Mrs. Manresa laughed. She remembered. An anecdote was on the tip of her tongue, about a public lavatory built to celebrate the same occasion, and how the Mayor ..... Could she tell it? No. The old lady, gazing at the swallows, looked too refined.   (p. 122)

This 'refeened' lady—'Mrs. Manresa qualified the word to her own advantage'—gazes beyond the clouds at 'blue, pure blue, black blue; blue that had never filtered down' (p. 30). This pure blue, like blue in art which signifies 'spiritual entity',[1] and is an 'image of totality',[2] becomes a symbol of 'God there, God on his throne' (p. 31). Seeing and feeling that 'God is Peace. God is Love', Mrs. Swithin symbolizes a devout Christian, a living abiding faith.

Similarly Virginia Woolf's treatment of the Rev. G. W. Streatfield in *Between the Acts* has undergone a significant change from that of Mr. Bax in *The Voyage Out*. Whereas Mr. Bax, 'the stout black figure' that 'passed through the hall with a preoccupied expression, as though he would rather not recognize salutations' (p. 274), is a little stand-offish, Mr. Streatfield with his forefinger 'stained with tobacco juice', being the representative of his flock, 'their symbol; themselves', comes nearer them and is able to communicate better. Mr. Bax hemmed in the four walls of the chapel, and true to his temper, talks about suspicion, animosity, and invokes the awful God to take revenge.

'Be merciful unto me, O God', he read, 'for man goeth about to devour me ..... They daily mistake my words: all that they imagine is to do me evil ..... Break their teeth, O God, in their mouths; smite the jaw-bones of the lions, O God .....   (*The Voyage Out*, p. 276)

Mr. Streatfield, on the other hand, speaks under the open skies, and talks 'as one of the audience' about understanding, love and unity, about our acting different parts but being the same, and about the fundamental unity not only between man and man, but also between man and all the creation: 'May we not hold that there is a spirit that inspires, pervades .....' (p. 224). Thus Mr. Streatfield, in contrast to Mr. Bax, becomes a symbol of what Virginia Woolf seems to think is Christianity adapted to the needs of the time, and of 'a simplified' Christian

[1] Herman Leicht, *History of the World's Art*, London, 1952, p. 306.
[2] *Van Gogh—Fifty Reproductions in Full Colour*, London, 1951, p. 34.

faith for which men like Harnack, and Stopford Brooke were making eloquent pleas.[1]

Besides Mrs. Swithin and Mr. Streatfield, Virginia Woolf has used other characters in this novel to evoke certain ideas. In contrast to Mrs. Swithin, who is full of faith, her brother, Mr. Oliver, is the doubting one.

> Fish had faith, she reasoned. They trust us because we've never caught 'em. But her brother would reply: 'That's greed.' 'Their beauty!' she protested. 'Sex,' he would say. 'Who makes sex susceptible to beauty?' she would argue. He shrugged who? Why? .....
> He would carry the torch of reason till it went out in the darkness of the cave. For herself, every morning, kneeling, she protected her vision. Every night she opened the window and looked at leaves against the sky. Then slept. Then the random ribbon of birds' voices woke her.   (p. 240)

He not only had said 'umbrellas' when she had said 'pray', but also names as 'greed' what she thinks is 'trust', and what she feels is 'beauty' he calls 'sex'. In answer to the argument of Mrs. Swithin, who keeps her faith alive, her brother shrugs his shoulders thus implying that reason has no answer to certain questions and that it leads to a blind alley, into the darkness of the cave. Virginia Woolf once more, as she had already done in *To the Lighthouse*, stresses the incapacity of intellect to reach Z—glimmering red in the distance.

Like Mr. Ramsay in *To the Lighthouse*, Mr. Oliver in *Between the Acts* is cold and hard-hearted. He is unmindful of the feelings and happiness of others. Mr. Ramsay destroyed all James's hopes by saying that it would not be fine enough to go to the lighthouse next day; Mr. Oliver destroys the innocent world of his grandson by terrifying him by wearing a mask:

> The little boy had lagged and was grouting in the grass ..... George grubbed. The flower blazed between the angles of the roots. Membrane after membrane was torn. It blazed a soft yellow, a lambent light under a film of velvet; it filled the caverns behind the eyes with light. All that inner darkness became a hall, leaf smelling, earth smelling of yellow light. And the tree was beyond the flower; the grass, the flower and the tree were entire. Down on his knees

[1] As reported by David Thomson in *The New Cambridge Modern History*, Vol. XII, 1960, p. 144, and as mentioned in the Foreword to *Die to Live* by Stopford A. Brooke, London 1924, p. v, respectively.

grubbing he held the flower complete. Then there was a roar and a hot breath and a stream of coarse grey hair rushed between him and the flower. Up he leapt, toppling in his fright, and saw coming towards him a terrible peaked eyeless monster moving on legs, brandishing arms.   (pp. 16–17)

Mr. Oliver destroyed this innocent world of grass, flower and trees, full of sweet smells and lambent lights, at whose heart there was for George a 'flower complete'. Mr. Oliver then took pleasure in teasing Isa:

'Your little boy's a cry-baby,' he said scornfully .....
'And he howled. He's a coward, your boy is.'
She frowned. He was not a coward, her boy wasn't. And she loathed the domestic, the possessive; the maternal. And he knew it and did it on purpose to tease her, the old brute, her father-in-law.
(pp. 25–26)

He also behaved brutishly towards Mrs. Swithin. When she was a child, he forced her to take the fish 'with gills full of blood' off the hook, and then growled 'Cindy' as she cried out, shocked by the blood. (p. 28).

This growling old man, who prefers *The Times* to books: 'the treasured life-blood of immortal spirits. Poets; the legis-lators of mankind' (p. 138), is unable to discriminate. He is easily taken in by the sham glitter of Mrs. Manresa, who restored his 'spice islands' to him (p. 52). Unlike Cobbet, the simple gardener, he is unable to see through 'the little game of the woman following the man' (p. 132). He who had himself used reason to refute Mrs. Swithin, thus demonstrates the limitations of the intellect which he himself has already admitted.

Besides Mrs. Swithin and Mr. Oliver, there are others in the book who are symbolic characters. Mrs. Manresa, the 'old strumpet' (p. 115) as Isa calls her, is a type one does not very much fancy (p. 187). She ogles Bart, the father. She flirts with Giles, the son. She even ogles Candish, the butler (p. 51). Thus ogling indiscriminately and vulgar in her gesture and in her whole person, over-sexed and over-dressed, she becomes to Giles in his rage, symbolic of lust (p. 118).

Giles Oliver is symbolically dressed as a cricketer. In the presence of Mrs. Manresa, who felt herself to be a queen, he was 'the surly hero' (p. 112). He is afraid of not being manly.

While going to the Barn to have tea, he takes the short cut by the fields.

This dry summer the path was strewn with stones. He kicked—a flinty yellow stone ..... Stone-kicking was a child's game. He remembered the rules.   (p. 118)

His kicking the stone is a symbolic act. It suggests not only his irritability, but also, being a child's game, his not being manly. He was feeling frustrated when he saw a snake choked in its effort to swallow a toad. 'The snake was unable to swallow; the toad was unable to die' (p. 119). He stamped on them, and his tennis shoes were stained with blood. 'But it was action.' Thus Giles unconsciously and symbolically proves to himself that he can act, and that he is a man able to impress Mrs. Manresa. On seeing his bloodstained shoes, she feels 'flattered'. She feels that he had done it to prove 'his valour for her admiration' (p. 128).

Again, Isa's plucking and then dropping of a flower has symbolic value.

'Now may I pluck,' Isa murmured, picking a rose, 'my single flower. The white or the pink? And press it so, twixt thumb and finger .....'
She looked among the passing faces for the face of the man in grey. There he was for one second; but surrounded, inaccessible. And now vanished.
She dropped her flower.   (p. 181)

The picking of the flower suggests her desire to get hold of the man in grey—the gentleman farmer. But he, being well guarded by his wife, is inaccessible to her. This she realizes and drops him symbolically by dropping the flower.

Isa Oliver, unlike Katharine in *Night and Day* who kept her mathematics in poetry books, writes her poems 'in the book bound like an account book' (p. 21). Her writing poetry is symbolic of her being romantic, even though, being thick of waist and large of limb, she does not look like Sappho (p. 22). She thinks in rhymes. Her rhymes, unlike the verses quoted by Clarissa in *Mrs. Dalloway*, and by Mr. Ramsay in *To the Lighthouse*, are not symbolic of any very deep meanings. They are monologues that mainly reflect her unfulfilled desires. 'Where we know not, where we go not, neither know nor care

..... with a feather ..... flying mounting through the air' (p. 21), for instance, represents her desire to fly away from Pointz Hall with the gentleman farmer.

Every summer, for seven summers now, Isa had heard the same words; about the hammer and the nails; the pageant and the weather. Every year they said, would it be wet or fine; and every year it was—one or the other. The same chime followed the same chime ..... (p. 29)

This mechanical repetition of set phrases year after year is symbolic of the boredom that has set in there, and of which Isa has become conscious. She wants something exciting, something sensational. When she goes to the library, she runs her eyes along the books.

The Faerie Queene and Kinglake's *Crimea*; Keats and the *Kreutzer Sonata* ..... Yeats and Donne ..... The life of Garibaldi. The life of Lord Palmerston .....

None of them stopped her toothache. For her generation the newspaper was a book; and, as her father-in-law had dropped *The Times*, she took it and read: '..... The troopers told her the horse had a green tail; but she found it was just an ordinary horse. And they dragged her up to the barrack room where she was thrown upon a bed. Then one of the troopers removed part of her clothing, and she screamed and hit him about the face .....'

That was real ..... (pp. 26–27)

The picking up of *The Times* in preference to books—'the mirror of the soul', therefore, becomes symbolic, as in *Jacob's Room*, of the shallowness of mind which craves only for something exciting and stirring.

Isa's falling in love and marrying Giles, and her unfruitful affair with William Dodge are also described symbolically.

They had met first in Scotland, fishing—she from one rock, he from another. Her line had got tangled; she had given over, and had watched him with the stream rushing between his legs, casting, casting—until, like a thick ingot of silver bent in the middle, the salmon had leapt, had been caught, and she had loved him. (p. 60)

The line getting entangled, and the salmon leaping and being caught, become symbolic of Isa's getting entangled in love and getting married.

L

Similarly when Isa took away Dodge to show him the green-house,

> she sat down on a plank under the vine. And he sat beside her. The little grapes above them were green buds; the leaves thin and yellow as the web between birds' claws .....
> 'That was your son,' he said, 'in the Barn?'
> She had a daughter, too, she told him, in the cradle.
> 'And you—married?' she asked. From her tone he knew she guessed, as women always guessed, everything. They knew at once they had nothing to fear, nothing to hope.   (p. 135)

In contrast to the ripe grapes which Clara and Jacob gather together in *Jacob's Room*, the green buds of these little grapes, and the thin yellow leaves become symbolic of 'nothing to fear nothing to hope'—the state of the relationship between William and Isa.

Talking about Baudelaire's use of imagery of common life, T. S. Eliot says,

> It is not merely in the use of imagery of common life, not merely in the use of imagery of the sordid life of a great metropolis, but in the elevation of such imagery to the *first intensity*—presenting it as it is, and yet making it represent something much more than itself—that Baudelaire created a mode of release and expression for other men.[1]

In the same way Virginia Woolf, in the Pageant, not only presents historical and literary facts as they are, but also makes them represent something much more than they are, so that they become symbolic of her own ideas. Miss La Trobe, who produces the pageant in aid of the village church, like Lily Briscoe in *To the Lighthouse*, Hewet in *The Voyage Out*, and Orlando, reflecting as she does the joys and agonies of creation similar to those recorded by Virginia Woolf herself in her diary, symbolizes a creative mind. She is

> one who seethes wandering bodies and floating voices in a cauldron, and makes rise up from its amorphous mass a recreated world.
>   (p. 180)

She is like Hewet in *The Voyage Out* who, explaining his theory of the novel, says,

---

[1] *Selected Essays*, London, 1953, p. 426.

'We want to find out what's behind things, don't we?—Look at the lights down there, ... scattered about anyhow. Things I feel come to me like lights ... I want to combine them ... Have you ever seen fireworks that make figures? ... I want to make figures.'   (p. 266)

Miss La Trobe by combining things wants to recreate her vision of life, and through the pageant wants to suggest 'the things that lie beneath the semblance of the thing'.

Pointz Hall and 'the noble Barn' which had been built over seven hundred years ago, and which evoked in some memories of 'a great temple', like the broad-backed moor in *Jacob's Room* that had heard the 'plaint and belief and elegy ..... any time these five hundred years', give a sense of durability and become symbols of historical time against which Virginia Woolf shows the rise and fall of great houses, and the passing away of golden ages. Like the Parthenon in *Jacob's Room*, and the oak tree and the castle in *Orlando*, they also evoke a sense of the transitoriness of human life and show up the vanity and arrogance of individuals. Virginia Woolf also suggests short-lived earthly glory and vanity by mentioning the names of the actors taking part in the pageant side by side with what they represent—Phyllis Jones: England, 'A child new born Sprung from the sea' (p. 95); Hilda: England grown into a girl (p. 97); Eliza Clark, licensed to sell tobacco: Queen Elizabeth (p. 101); Mabel Hopkins: Reason—and so on. This not only imparts local colour to the pageant, but also emphasizes that they are Kings and Queens, and Dukes and Duchesses, for a short time only, and that, too, at the mere command of Miss La Trobe.

Then, at a sign from Miss La Trobe behind the tree, the dance stopped. A procession formed. Great Eliza descended from her soap box. Taking her skirt in her hand, striding with long strides, surrounded by Dukes and Princes, followed by the lovers arm in arm, with Albert the idiot playing in and out, and the corpse on its bier concluding the procession, the Elizabethan age passed from the scene.   (p. 113)

Thus demonstrating the transitoriness of Great Queens and memorable ages, the pageant becomes symbolic of the pageant of the world. As Virginia Woolf writes when commenting on the Elizabethan plays: 'The pageant of the world is marvellous, but the pageant of the world is vanity', and she goes on to quote:

> ..... glories
> Of human greatness are but pleasing dreams
> And shadows soon decaying .....[1]

If the world is a stage and all the men and women are 'merely players'—one of the ideas that this pageant symbolizes—then 'Whose play?' is the question that this pageant poses. 'Ah, that's the question', as one of the audience remarks (p. 233). Virginia Woolf, perhaps, by posing this question, is fortifying the faith that she has symbolized in Mrs. Swithin, that there is 'a prayable being controlling the thrush and the worm' who is directing the pageant of life.

Whereas on one plane Virginia Woolf seems to agree with what Prospero says in *The Tempest* about the great globe and all that it inherits which, fading away like the insubstantial pageant, shall 'Leave not a rack behind', on another plane she sees eternity beyond mutability. She seems to be of the opinion that whereas men and women change man remains unchanged. What she had said about the human spirit in *The Waves*, she says about humanity in *Between the Acts*. The villagers and peasants recurring in the different scenes of the pageant, like the chorus in a Greek play, not only connect the different scenes but also symbolize the elemental humanity that persists when the Kings and Queens, the Dukes and Lords, and the clown and the courtiers, pass away.

Digging and delving (they sang), *hedging and ditching we pass ... Summer and winter, autumn and spring return ... All passes but we, all changes ... but we remain for ever the same .....*

Palaces tumble down (they resumed), *Babylon, Nineveh, Troy ... And Caesar's great house ... all fallen they lie ... Where the plover nests was the arch ... through which the Romans trod ... Digging and delving we break with the share of the plough the clod ... Where Clytemnestra watched for her Lord ... saw the beacons blaze on the hills ... we see only the clod ... Digging and delving we pass ... and the Queen and the Watch Tower fall ... for Agamemnon has ridden away ... Clytemnestra is nothing but ...*   (p. 164)

These peasants, like the peasants and shepherds in Hardy's novels, symbolize elemental man who, devoid of painted pomp, show and greed, continues to earn his bread by the sweat of his

---

[1] *The Common Reader*, First Series, p. 82

brow, while mighty kings and their greedy courts, who thrive only by exploiting others, become like dust to dust returning.

The pageant, besides showing that the glories of this earth are, as the Preacher said, 'Vanity of vanities', suggests the passage of time and its continual change. As the 'leaden circles' caused by the strokes of Big Ben in *Mrs. Dalloway* measure out the irrevocable hours of present time, so the age of Chaucer, the Elizabethan Age, the Restoration period, and the Victorian Age in the pageant, like the names of kings and queens in *Orlando*, measure out historical time. Virginia Woolf also suggests time and change through Mrs. Swithin's reading of history.

She had been waked by the birds. How they sang! attacking the dawn like so many choir boys attacking an iced cake. Forced to listen, she had stretched for her favourite reading—an Outline of History—and had spent the hours between three and five thinking of rhododendron forests in Piccadilly; when the entire continent, not then, she understood, divided by a channel, was all one; populated, she understood, by elephant-bodied, seal-necked, heaving, surging, slowly writhing, and, she supposed, barking monsters; the iguanodon, the mammoth and the mastodon; from whom presumably, she thought, jerking the window open, we descend.

(p. 13)

Continuing her reading of the Outline of History in the evening, Mrs. Swithin read that England

'was then a swamp. Thick forests covered the land. On the top of their matted branches birds sang .....

'Prehistoric man', she read, 'half-human, half-ape roused himself from his semi-crouching position and raised great stones.'

(pp. 254-5)

Mrs. Swithin's reading of history, recalling prehistoric time and the evolution that life has undergone from iguanodons to modern man, gives us an insight into Virginia Woolf's ideas about time and change. In this she appears to share the view expressed by Wordsworth in 'The Prelude' that the 'Vast Frame of social nature' goes on changing 'With an ascent and progress in the main'.

The pageant, being a comic reconstruction of the social and literary history of England, comments in a light, humorous way on the modes and manners of different periods of history. While caricaturing facts Virginia Woolf uses them as symbols to suggest something more than what they are. Phyllis Jones, 'a small girl, like a rosebud in pink', represents early England. Hilda—the carpenter's daughter—who takes her place, suggests that 'England's grown'. The flowers in her hair, suggesting, as Mrs. Swithin says, that she had been 'maying and nutting', symbolize the age of Chaucer.

The villagers, while passing in and out between the trees, sing, '*to the shrine of the Saint . . . to the tomb . . . lovers . . . believers . . ., we come . . .*' After they have paid their homage, their singing changes to

> *I kissed a girl and let her go,*
> *Another did I tumble,*
> *In the straw and in the hay .....*   (pp. 98–99)

Their homage to the Saint and then their song about tumbling a girl in the hay portray the robust faith and the uninhibited pleasures of the age of Chaucer and the *Canterbury Tales*.

The next scene of the pageant represents the Elizabethan Age.

From behind the bushes issued Queen Elizabeth—Eliza Clark, licensed to sell tobacco ..... She was splendidly made up ..... And when she mounted the soap box in the centre, representing perhaps a rock in the ocean, her size made her appear gigantic.   (p. 101)

Eliza's looking 'gigantic' evokes the greatness of 'the great Queen' whose hand, as Virginia Woolf writes in *Orlando*, 'had only to raise itself for a head to fall' (p. 23). The play that is staged before her on her command, 'Play out the play', is a parody of Elizabethan drama. It represents Virginia Woolf's idea about 'the Elizabethan view of reality', as stated by her in 'Notes on an Elizabethan Play':

Exquisite is the delight, sublime the relief of being set free to wander in the land of the unicorn and the jeweller among dukes and grandees, Gonzaloes and Bellimperias, who spend their lives in murder and intrigue, dress up as men if they are women, as women if they are men, see ghosts, run mad, and die in the greatest profusion on the slightest provocation .....
(*The Common Reader*, First Series, p. 73)

The play has dukes and grandees, a girl disguised as a boy, and

all the usual intrigues. Death on the stage—an established
occurrence in an Elizabethan play—is represented by the
crone who 'fell back lifeless' at the end and was carried out on
a bier in a procession. Albert, the idiot, sententious like the
fool in *King Lear*, shouting,

> *I know, I know—*
> *What don't I know?*
> *All your secret, ladies,*
> *All yours too, gentlemen ...*   (p. 104)

is, as William says, 'in the tradition'. Besides parodying the
Elizabethan drama, the play represents its spirit.

She bawled. They bawled. All together they bawled and so
loud that it was difficult to make out what they were saying .....

Dukes, priests, shepherds, pilgrims and serving men took hands
and danced. The idiot scampered in and out. Hands joined, heads
knocking, they danced round the majestic figure of the Elizabethan
age personified by Mrs. Clark, licensed to sell tobacco, on her soap
box.

It was a mellay; a medley.   (pp. 108–12)

The bawling and dancing of the actors signifies the bawling
vigour of the Elizabethan drama about which Virginia Woolf
says:

There is, even in the worst, an intermittent bawling vigour which
gives us the sense in our quiet arm-chairs of ostlers and orange-girls
catching up the lines, flinging them back, hissing or stamping
applause.   (*The Common Reader*, First Series, p. 75)

Similarly the second play of the pageant, 'Where there's a
Will, there's a Way', is a delightful comment on the Restoration Drama. The characters in this play, Sir Spaniel Lilyliver,
Lady Harpy Harraden, and Valentine, like many of the
characters in Restoration plays, are types portraying various
characteristics. Lady Harpy Harraden, as her name implies, is a
grasping, haggard old vixen. 'Pointing the finger of scorn',
Flavinda rightly called her an old woman. She wants Sir Spaniel
to marry Flavinda on the condition 'that the money is shared
between us', (p. 157). Spaniel Lilyliver, also, is true to his name.
So long as he thinks that he can marry Flavinda with the help
of Lady Harpy, he pays the latter compliments like a gallant in

love. No sooner does he come to know that the marriage is not possible than he appears in his true colours. He utters outright what he used to whisper in asides before. She whom he described as the sun before whom the Cassiopeias, Aldebarans, Great Bears—the lesser lights—were not worth a fig, becomes worse than 'a tar barrel' and 'a thorn tree' (pp. 153, 171). He cannot stand up for his love and honour. It is only when Flavinda and Valentine have gone away to Gretna Green that Sir Spaniel wishes that he 'could braise 'em in a mortar and serve 'em up smoking hot on the altar of —' (p. 169). 'Where there's a Will, there's a Way' resembles Congreve's *The Way of the World* not only in its plot but also in its wealth of figures and imagery, and its coarse language and extravagant humour.

The scene which is set for this play is typical of the period:

Then while [Reason] gazed, helpers from the bushes arranged round her what appeared to be the three sides of a room. In the middle they stood a table. On the table they placed a china tea service. Reason surveyed this domestic scene from her lofty eminence unmoved.

(p. 149)

The three sides of a room represent a drawing-room on the stage. It suggests the elaborate sets within the proscenium arch that had developed during this period. The china tea service signifies not only the new manners and customs of the period but also the drawing-room nature of the Restoration comedy.

The Victorian Age in the next scene of the pageant is symbolized by Budge.

And once more a huge symbolical figure emerged from the bushes. It was Budge the publican ..... He wore a long black, many-caped cloak; waterproof; shiny; of the substance of a statue in Parliament Square; a helmet which suggested a policeman; a row of medals crossed his breast; and in his right hand, he held extended a special constable's baton.

(p. 188)

This fine figure of a Victorian constable with his extended baton becomes a symbol of the enforcement of 'the laws of God and Man' in 'our Empire; under the White Queen Victoria'. Virginia Woolf conveys her 'sneer' against the Victorian age through Budge who ironically mentions 'the price of Empire ..... the white man's burden', and through Etty Springett who thinks about the basements and the divorced

ladies who were not received at court—subjects amply com-
mented upon by the author in *A Room of One's Own*, *The Years*,
and *Three Guineas*.

Mrs. Hardcastle, the Victorian matron, 'with children, young
men, young women ..... ', who arrive for the picnic, represents,
as Virginia Woolf says in *Three Guineas*, the intensive child-
bearing unpaid wife. She is a symbol of the average Victorian
woman whom Virginia Woolf caricatured in *Orlando*: 'The life
of the average woman was a succession of childbirths. She
married at nineteen and had fifteen or eighteen children by
the time she was thirty; for twins abounded' (p. 207).

After the popping of the corks, the slicing of grouse, ham,
and chicken, when 'the chump of jaws and the chink of glasses'
had ceased, the young ladies were called upon to sing.

Mrs. H. (authoritatively). *Eleanor and Mildred will now sing 'I'd be a
Butterfly'.*
(Eleanor and Mildred rise obediently and sing a duet: 'I'd be a
Butterfly.')
Mrs. H. *Thank you very much, my dears. And now gentlemen, Our Country!*
(Arthur and Edgar sing 'Rule, Britannia'.)   (pp. 198–9)

Mrs. Hardcastle's authoritative command and the obedience of
the girls are symbolic of the enforcement of paternal authority in
Victorian homes just as Budge's extended baton is symbolic
of the enforcement of the law in Victoria's country. Similarly
Virginia Woolf makes the singing of the two popular songs of
the period, 'I'd be a Butterfly' by the young ladies, and 'Rule,
Britannia' by the young men, symbolic of what young men
and young women were supposed to do in later life. Whereas
the young men were prepared to rule the Empire, the daughters, as Virginia Woolf writes in *A Room of One's Own* and *Three
Guineas*, were not allowed to join the professions. They were
supposed to be like butterflies during the season, to be caught,
and become the unpaid wives and house-keepers for the bread-
winner.

The suppression of women, the pushing down to the basement of servants, the sweating at the mines and the coughing
at the looms of the poor and their festering in 'Cripplegate,
St. Giles, Whitechapel', Virginia Woolf feels, were the inherent
seeds of corruption—something unhygienic about the home,

M

'like a bit of meat gone sour', as Mrs. Lynn-Jones expressed it —that made Victorian glory perish.

The last scene of the pageant—'The present time. Ourselves' —epitomizes her message and is highly symbolical. It starts as Isa cries, 'O look'.

> That was a ladder. And that (a cloth roughly painted) was a wall. And that a man with a hod on his back.   (p. 211)

Virginia Woolf explains these symbols through Mr. Page, the reporter, who, licking his pencil, notes:

> With the very limited means at her disposal, Miss La Trobe con-veyed to the audience Civilization (the wall) in ruins; rebuilt (witness man with hod) by human effort; witness also woman handing bricks.   (p. 212)

The woman handing bricks signifies that women in the present age, unlike women in the Victorian era, are working side by side with men. Will their effort be fruitful? Will they be able to rebuild civilization?

> Each flat with its refrigerator, in the crannied wall. Each of us a free man; plates washed by machinery; not an aeroplane to vex us; all liberated; made whole.   (p. 213)

Virginia Woolf seems to say that so long as we remain what the mirrors held up by the children show us to be, 'orts, scraps, fragments', we shall never be able to rebuild civilization.

> Look! Out they come, from the bushes—the riff-raff. Children? Imps—elves—demons. Holding what? ..... Anything that's bright enough to reflect, presumably, ourselves? .....
> Here a nose ... There a skirt ... Then trousers only ... Now per-haps a face ... Ourselves? But that's cruel. To snap us as we are, before we've had time to assume ...   (p. 214)

The flashing of the mirrors by the children shatters the leth-argic complacency of the older generation by showing them up without giving them time to assume and be hypocritical, to prepare faces. As Baudelaire in his poem 'To the Reader', by calling 'the filthy, foul and evil' reader his twin brother and a humbug, wants to show the *ennui* of the age, Virginia Woolf, by reflecting the audience in the mirrors, tries to show them what they had become. The mirrors reflect us as we are

Ourselves ..... Liars most of us. Thieves too ..... The poor are as bad as the rich are. Perhaps worse. Don't hide among rags. Or let our cloth protect us. Or for the matter of that book learning; or skilful practice on pianos; or laying on of paint ..... Consider the gun slayers, bomb droppers here or there. They do openly what we do slyly.
(p. 218)

The ills of the world, Virginia Woolf feels, are due less to the gun slayers and the bomb droppers, who do it openly, than to ourselves, who do worse things slyly, having lost our 'innocency', 'faith in love', and 'virtue'. Our fine clothes and mastery of the arts cannot hide us, when our actions betray us.

Take for example ..... Mr. M's bungalow. A view spoilt for ever. That's murder ... Or Mrs. E's lipstick and blood-red nails ... A tyrant, remember, is half a slave. Item, the vanity of Mr. H. the writer ... Then there's the amiable condescension of the lady of the manor ... and buying shares in the market to sell 'em ... Look at ourselves, ladies and gentlemen! Then at the wall; and ask how's this wall, the great wall, which we call, perhaps miscall, civilization, to be built by ... orts, scraps and fragments like ourselves?
(pp. 218-19)

Mr. M., Mrs. E., Mr. H., the lady of the manor, and the speculator, all symbolize selfishness, vanity, a sense of superiority, greed, and love of exploitation—the vices that divide man from man. So long as we indulge in these vices we shall remain individualistic and disunited—orts, scraps and fragments. We shall not be able to understand the 'real life', which, as Virginia Woolf says in *A Room of One's Own*, is the 'common life', and not the little separate life of an individual (p. 17). We shall not become wholes till we, realizing with the Apostle Paul that God 'created every race of men of one stock, to inhabit the whole earth's surface', stop feeling superior and calling 'profane what God counts clean'.[1] This seems to be Virginia Woolf's message to warring humanity, to the different nations that fight each other. To rebuild civilization, we have to understand the basic brotherhood of man. We have to realize that, as the pageant conveyed to the Rev. G. W. Streatfield, 'we act different parts; but are the same', that not only human life but all the creation is the same.

'Dare we, I ask myself, limit life to ourselves? May we not hold that there is a spirit that inspires, pervades.
(p. 224)

[1] *The New English Bible*, Acts of the Apostles 17.26 and 11.9.

Thus Mr. Streatfield, who like Mrs. Swithin wears a cross, feels like her that there is an all pervading presence.

> Mrs. Swithin caressed her cross. She gazed vaguely at the view. She was off, they guessed, on a circular tour of the imagination— one-making. Sheep, cows, grass, trees, ourselves—all are one.
>
> (p. 204)

Besides men, women, children and the idiot, cows, swallows, martins, and even trees, participate in the pageant. When 'the illusion petered out, the cows took up the burden'. They started bellowing and thus

> annihilated the gap; bridged the distance; filled the emptiness and continued the emotion.
>
> Miss La Trobe waved her hand ecstatically at the cows.
>
> 'Thank Heaven!' she exclaimed.   (pp. 165-6)

Similarly the dancing swallows and the trees become an integral part of the pageant.

> Suddenly the tune stopped. The tune changed. A waltz, was it? Something half known, half not. The swallows danced it. Round and round, in and out they skimmed. Real swallows. Retreating and advancing. And the trees, O the trees, how gravely and sedately like senators in council, or the spaced pillars of some cathedral church ..... The temple-haunting martins who come, have always come.   (pp. 212-13)

Thus the bellowing cows and the dancing swallows, becoming active participants in the pageant, symbolize the basic unity and the oneness of all life.

The oneness of all life Virginia Woolf again suggests by using the fish and the insects symbolically. When Mrs. Swithin gazed at the lily pool,

> something moved in the water; her favourite fantail. The golden orfe followed. Then she had a glimpse of silver—the great carp himself, who came to the surface so very seldom. They slid on, in and out between the stalks, silver; pink; gold; splashed; streaked; pied.
>
> 'Ourselves', she murmured. And retrieving some glint of faith from the grey waters, hopefully, without much help from reason, she followed the fish; the speckled, streaked and blotched; seeing in vision beauty, power, and glory in ourselves.   (pp. 239-40)

The fish is, as Jessie Weston says in *From Ritual to Romance*, a life symbol of immemorial antiquity. The different coloured species of fish, like the various sized clouds in *The Waves*, suggesting different types of persons, become symbolic of life. Mrs. Swithin, recognizing that the fish are like 'ourselves' sees a oneness in life. And this similarity of pattern between life among men, and life among birds and beasts is again hinted at when Virginia Woolf sets their actions side by side.

There in that hollow of the sun-baked field were congregated the grasshopper, the ant, and the beetle, rolling pebbles of sun-baked earth through the glistening stubble. In that rosy corner of the sun-baked field Bartholomew, Giles and Lucy polished and nibbled and broke off crumbs.   (p. 253)

Instead of using the insects sarcastically to disparage human character, as she does in *The Voyage Out*, Virginia Woolf here points out the similarity of action between the two strata of the animal kingdom, and so demonstrates the unity and oneness of the whole creation.

The pageant, even though drawn from the history of the British Isles, and portraying the development of the English nation, becomes symbolic of the evolution of the whole human race. Virginia Woolf achieves this by subtle suggestions of other nations and continents. Mr. Page, reporting the pageant, notes,

Now issued black man in fuzzy wig; coffee coloured ditto in silver turban; they signify presumably the League of ...   (p. 212)

And when Mrs. Swithin was gazing at the lily pool,

the jagged leaf at the corner suggested, by its contours, Europe. There were other leaves. She fluttered her eye over the surface, naming leaves India, Africa, America. Islands of security, glossy and thick.   (p. 239)

The mention of the black man with fuzzy wig and the coffee coloured man with a silvery turban, representing other races and nationalities, of leaves with contours resembling India, Africa, and America, suggesting other countries and continents, brings within the circle of one-making all lands and all people, and enlarges the circumference till it becomes all-encompassing.

Thus in this delightful (not, surely 'most unhappy'[1]) book, I feel, Virginia Woolf has achieved even more than what she originally set out to do when she wrote in her diary:

Why not *Poyntzet Hall*: a centre: all literature discussed in connection with real little incongruous living humour: and anything that comes into my head; but 'I' rejected: 'We' substituted: to whom at the end there shall be an invocation? 'We' ... the composed of many different things ... we all life, all art, all waifs and strays—a rambling capricious but somehow unified whole—the present state of my mind?[2]

[1] Philip Rahv: *Image and Idea*, N.Y., 1957, p. 169.
[2] *Diary*, pp. 289–90.

Bibliography

ANNAN, NOEL, *Leslie Stephen*, London, 1951.

BELL, CLIVE, *Old Friends*, London, 1956.

BENNETT, ARNOLD, *The Savour of Life*, London, 1928.

BENNETT, JOAN, *Virginia Woolf—Her Art as a Novelist*, Cambridge, 1949.

BERGSON, HENRI, *An Introduction to Metaphysics*, London, 1913.

BLACKSTONE, BERNARD, *Virginia Woolf, a Commentary*, London, 1949.

BOWEN, ELIZABETH, *English Novelists*, London, 1942.

—— *Collected Impressions*, London, 1950.

BOWRA, C. M., *The Heritage of Symbolism*, London, 1943.

BREWSTER, DOROTHY and BURRELL, ANGUS, *Modern Fiction*, N.Y., 1934.

BURGUM, EDWIN BERRY, *The Novel and the World's Dilemma*, N.Y., 1947.

CASSIRER, E., *An Essay on Man*, Yale University Press, 1944.

CECIL, DAVID, *Poets and Story-Tellers*, London, 1949.

COMPTON-RICKETT, A., *Portraits and Personalities*, London, 1937.

DAICHES, DAVID, *The Novel and the Modern World*, Chicago University Press, 1939.

—— *Virginia Woolf*, London, 1945.

DREW, ELIZABETH, *The Modern Novel*, London, 1926.

FORSTER, E. M., *Virginia Woolf*, Cambridge, 1942.

GARNETT, DAVID, *The Flowers of the Forest*, London, 1955.

GRUBBER, RUTH, *Virginia Woolf—a Study*, Leipzig, 1935.

HAFLEY, JAMES, *The Glass Roof—Virginia Woolf as Novelist*, University of California Press, 1954.

HOARE, DOROTHY M., *Some Studies in the Modern Novel*, London, 1938.

HOLTBY, WINIFRED, *Virginia Woolf*, London, 1932.

JOHNSON, R. BRIMLEY, *Some Contemporary Novelists* (Women), London, 1920.

JOHNSTONE, J. K., *The Bloomsbury Group*, London, 1959.

LANGER, S. K., *Feeling and Form*, London, 1953.

LEWIS, WYNDHAM, *Men Without Art*, London, 1934.

MAITLAND, FREDERIC W., *The Life and Letters of Sir Leslie Stephen*, London, 1906.

MANSFIELD, KATHERINE, *Novels and Novelists*, London, 1930.

MULLER, HERBERT J., *Modern Fiction, A Study of Values*, London, 1937.
NEWTON, DEBORAH, *Virginia Woolf*, Melbourne University Press, 1946.
RANTAVAARA, IRMA, *Virginia Woolf and Bloomsbury*, Helsinki, 1953.
SACKVILLE-WEST, V., *Knole and the Sackvilles*, London, 1922.
SPENDER, STEPHEN, *World Within World*, London, 1951.
SYMONS, ARTHUR, *The Symbolist Movement in Literature*, London, 1899.
TINDALL, W. Y., *Forces in Modern British Literature 1885–1946*, N.Y., 947.
—— *The Literary Symbol*, N.Y., 1955.
URBAN, W. M., *Language and Reality*, London, 1939.
WHITEHEAD, A. N., *Symbolism: Its Meaning and Effect*, Cambridge, 1928.
WILSON, EDMUND, *Axel's Castle, A Study in the Imaginative Literature of 1870–1930*, N.Y., 1931.

Note: B. J. Kirkpatrick's *A Bibliography of Virginia Woolf*, London, 1957, 'Criticism of Virginia Woolf: a Selected Checklist' in *Modern Fiction Studies* II, i, 1956, and James Hafley's *The Glass Roof: Virginia Woolf as Novelist*, University of California Press, 1954 give detailed bibliographies of Virginia Woolf's own writings and of criticism of her works.

Index